THE
MEDIATOR'S
APPROACH

THE
MEDIATOR'S
APPROACH

Five *(and A Half)* Paths Through Conflict

TARA WEST

Copyright © 2021 Tara West

All rights reserved. No part of this book may be reproduced, or stored in a retrieval system, or transmitted in any form or by any means, electronic, mechanical, photocopying, recording, or otherwise, without express written permission of the publisher.

ISBN: 979-8-5175-9046-6

Design: Mercedes Piñera

TABLE OF CONTENTS

PREFACE 9

1. YOU CAN CHOOSE YOUR APPROACH 13
   Four mediation goals 15
      Goal 1: Reach an agreement 15
      Goal 2: Reach a high-quality agreement 15
      Goal 3: Reach a high-quality outcome (other than an agreement) 16
      Goal 4: Participate in a high-quality process 16
   Mediation defined 18
   Five (and a half) approaches to mediation 19

2. EVALUATIVE MEDIATION 25
   The Dealmakers' theory and goals 26
   How do the Dealmakers do it? 27
      Share selective evaluations of each party's case 27
      Caucus 27
      Anything and everything 29
   The Judges' theory and goals 30
   How do the Judges do it? 31
      Straight up, tell the parties what they should do 31
      A smorgasbord of practices, unless and until the mediator sees a problem 32
   Ironies and explanations of evaluative mediation 35

3. FACILITATIVE MEDIATION 45
Theory and goals 45
How do they do it? 46
Establishing ground Rules 47
Normalizing 47
Reframing 48
Emphasizing common ground 48
Mutualizing 49
Focusing on the future 49
Interest-based problem-solving 50
Theory and goals, revisited 52

4. TRANSFORMATIVE MEDIATION 57
Theory and goals 57
How do they do it? 62
The opening statement 62
Reflection 63
Summary 66
Check-In 67
Theory and goals, revisited 70

5. UNDERSTANDING-BASED MEDIATION 77
Theory and goals 77
How do they do it? 81
Looping 82
Contracting 84
Defining the problem 85
Working through the conflict 86
Developing and evaluating options 86
Reaching agreement 90

Theory and goals, revisited 91

6. NARRATIVE MEDIATION 97
Theory and goals 97
How do they do it? 100
The engagement phase 100
Deconstructing the conflict-saturated story 101
Constructing the alternative story 104
Theory and goals, revisited 106

7. NEXT STEPS 111
A brief recap 111
Evaluative Mediation...112
Facilitative Mediation 112
Transformative Mediation 113
Understanding-Based Mediation..113
Narrative Mediation 114
And the winner is… 115
A few recommendations...116

REFERENCES 121

ADDITIONAL RESOURCES 133

ABOUT THE AUTHOR 135

PREFACE

Why write a book about mediation approaches? Or rather, why did I write a book about mediation approaches? For the ten years that I've been studying, teaching, and practicing in the field of conflict resolution, I've had a love-hate relationship with mediation. At times, I felt like mediation could save the world - it satisfied my inner peacemaker's desire to bring people together in a spirit of understanding and cooperation, allowing them to find win-win solutions while improving their relationships. At other times, I thought it was a scam - it violated my inner lawyer's desire for justice, as it seemed to remove the protections and oversight of legal precedent that took years to develop, allowing unscrupulous people to achieve one-sided victories. Eventually I concluded that mediation could be all of this and more, depending on the parties, the situation, and, perhaps most importantly, the mediator's approach - their chosen path through conflict.

So I wrote the book that I would have been eager to read when first embarking on this journey. I wrote this to equip you, the fledgling mediator, with a better understanding of the many ways that mediation is practiced, and why. With this knowledge, you will be in the best position to make choices that are right for you, putting you on a path toward a successful and rewarding career as a mediator.

This project would not have been possible without the generous support of others. I want to express my heartfelt thanks to my family, friends, and colleagues who offered their thoughtful feedback, along with their encouragement to continue moving forward. The insightful comments of Ken Sandbank, Pamela Struss, Amy Stevens, Joan Butler, Jeff Parks, and Diane West undoubtedly improved the quality of my thinking and writing. I greatly appreciate the generosity and contributions of each of these readers.

And I owe a special debt of gratitude to my mediation trainer, colleague, and friend, Dan Simon. Dan not only read and commented on multiple drafts of this book, he also inspired and shaped my views of what mediation could offer. This would be a very different book, and I would be a very different mediator, without Dan's wisdom and support.

Finally, I want to thank all the mediation trainers, co-mediators, workshop participants, students, and clients I've had the privilege to work with over the years. I learned something from every one of you. Thank you for your patience as I discovered how much more there was to learn.

Tara West
July 2021

1. YOU CAN CHOOSE YOUR APPROACH

If you've not yet taken your first mediation training, kudos to you for doing your research from the get-go. If you're reading this after taking a training (or two, or five, or…), you are very likely aware that mediation trainers are some of the loveliest people you'll ever meet. And these lovely people are introducing you to an even lovelier world – a world where conflicts lead to honest communication, connections are forged in place of war, and win-win solutions trump lose-lose struggles – a world you'll want to be a part of. You will fall in love with the people who bring you this religion of mediation, and you'll be tempted to treat the words of your new saviors as gospel.

And if you happened to choose the right mediation approach for you, this all may work out splendidly. However, if you're like me, you probably did not do a lot of research before taking your first mediation training, and you may not have even realized that there were multiple approaches to choose from. Because there are many different approaches to mediation, people who call themselves mediators often mean very different things by the term. And to make things even more confusing, there are sometimes large differences *within* approaches. This will be true for some approaches more than others because some are more clearly defined than others, as you'll soon see.

Why might you want to understand mediation approaches? If you're reading this book, you've undoubtedly heard about the many benefits of mediation, including that mediation offers people the opportunity to make their own decisions and potentially save time, money, and relationships, particularly when compared to litigation. However, research on mediation's benefits (and harms), for society and for the parties,[1] in addition to the mediator,[2] has yielded mixed results.

While a number of relevant factors are out of the mediator's control, the mediator's approach likely plays a role in mediation's effects on all involved. Differences in the ways that mediators practice are not subtle. Although there is some overlap across many of the approaches, there are also approaches that directly contradict each other. For example, one mediation trainer will tell you it's a good idea to emphasize the positive (e.g., what's working in the relationship, what the parties can agree on), and focus on the future (what they would like to see going forward); while another mediation trainer will say you should not guide the parties at all, but should instead follow them along the path they choose, which may include focusing on the past and everything that's gone wrong between them.

How can this be? What explains the differences between mediators, who all are trying to accomplish the same thing? Well, it turns out that mediators are not all trying to accomplish the same thing, at least not directly. So before we talk about the different ways mediators practice, let's talk about the different goals mediators are aiming for. What are they trying to accomplish?

FOUR MEDIATION GOALS

Four goals many mediators have for the parties, but prioritize differently, are: 1) Reach an agreement (any agreement); 2) reach a high-quality agreement; 3) reach a high-quality outcome (other than an agreement); and 4) participate in a high-quality process.

Goal 1: Reach an agreement

Many people assume that helping the parties reach an agreement is the top priority for all mediators. Although all mediators would undoubtedly prefer this outcome, all things being equal, not every mediator prioritizes or even aims at this goal. Mediators who do prioritize this goal view it as their job to get the parties to settle by (almost) any means necessary.[3]

Goal 2: Reach a high-quality agreement

Some mediators prioritize the *quality* of the agreement over the agreement itself. These mediators might strive for an agreement, but they have certain standards for the agreement (e.g., that the agreement is fair, durable, and/or close to what a judge might order); and these standards are more important to the mediator than simply reaching an agreement.[4] So mediators who value the quality of the agreement would rather see the parties leave mediation *without* an agreement than see them reach an agreement the mediator thinks is problematic. As you might imagine, different mediators use different criteria when judging the quality of the agreement.

Goal 3: Reach a high-quality outcome (other than an agreement)

Some mediators aim for and prioritize outcomes *other* than agreements. For example, some strive for harmonious or respectful relations between the parties, with the agreement being a secondary concern.[5] Others aim for mutual understanding between the parties,[6] whereas other mediators try to help each party become more empowered throughout the process.[7] As you can see, in the same way a high-quality *agreement* varies across mediators, a high-quality *outcome* can also take different forms for different mediators.

Goal 4: Participate in a high-quality process

Mediators who prioritize the quality of the process might hope (and believe) the process will lead to positive outcomes for the parties, but they are not focusing on those outcomes during the process itself.[8] Neither are they measuring success by typical outcome-related benchmarks, likely because these mediators do not assume they know what a high-quality outcome will look like in any particular situation. In some cases, it might be an agreement; in others, it may not.

As you may have guessed, the definition of a high-quality process also varies across mediators. Mediators who prioritize the quality of the process measure success by what the mediator does (e.g., reflect the parties accurately), by what the parties do (e.g., communicate openly and respectfully), or by what the parties and mediator do together (e.g., the parties participate in a brainstorming session led by the mediator).

As I mentioned earlier, some mediators only value one of these goals, while others value two, three, or even all four of these goals. What largely differentiates mediators is the weight they give to each goal and how they use the goals to guide them during the process. And while there are many possible reasons for the different goals (e.g., different assumptions about conflict and human nature, different professional backgrounds), the lack of a single, agreed-upon definition of mediation likely plays a role.

MEDIATION DEFINED

Definitions of mediation largely fall into three categories: 1) those that emphasize the goal of helping the parties reach an agreement (e.g., "Mediation is an informal process in which a neutral third party – known as a Mediator – helps you and the other party reach an agreement on some or all of your differences"[9]); 2) those that emphasize helping the parties communicate, while alluding to the goal of reaching an agreement (e.g., "Mediation is an alternative dispute resolution [ADR] process in which a trained neutral mediator facilitates communication between the parties and, without deciding the issues or imposing a solution on the parties, enables them to understand and to reach a mutually agreeable resolution to their dispute"[10]); and 3) those that emphasize communication and decision-making, without referencing an agreement or resolution at all (e.g., "Mediation is a process in which an impartial third party facilitates communication and negotiation and promotes voluntary decision making by the parties to the dispute"[11]).

The definition of mediation has been the focus of much debate, perhaps because the way mediation is defined will likely affect the goals, and therefore practices, of the mediator.[12] And mediators can get very attached to their own goals and practices!

FIVE (AND A HALF) APPROACHES TO MEDIATION

Many of these collections of goals and practices (a.k.a. approaches) have labels, but there is no clear agreement on how to differentiate one approach from another, or what some of the labels even mean.[13] This is made more complicated by the fact that many mediators refer to their approach as "eclectic,"[14] or simply refrain from labeling it at all.[15]

In this book, I'll use the labels you'll most often hear in the field, and I'll talk about the different ways these labels are used. This will familiarize you with the terms, and with what mediators actually do, regardless of the labels they're using. With this, you'll have a roadmap to the mediation world, and a way to understand the language spoken by its inhabitants.

First, I'll cover the "Big Three" mediation approaches, which everyone in the field seems to know by name – evaluative, facilitative, and transformative. Of these, only the transformative approach is a mediation *model*, meaning there is a foundational text that clearly spells out the theory, goals, values, and practices of the approach.[16] The evaluative and facilitative approaches are instead broad labels used to group a collection of practices that actually exist along a continuum.[17] In fact, the evaluative approach is so inconsistently defined that I'm calling it an approach and a half. Just try and stop me.

Next, I will cover the understanding-based[18] and narrative[19] approaches. I'm including these largely because, like the transformative approach, they are mediation *models*. Covering these models will help clarify connections between theory and practice that are likely present, if implicit, in the other approaches, as well.

This is not an exhaustive list, but having a handle on these five (and a half!) approaches to mediation will take you a long way toward understanding the range of practices that mediators use, and why. So now let's begin our tour with an approach to mediation that you're probably familiar with, even if you didn't know its name, and that's evaluative mediation.

1   See Beck, C. J. A., Sales, B. D., & Emery, R. E. (2004). Research on the impact of family mediation. In J. Folberg, A. L. Milne, & P. Salem (Eds.), *Divorce and family mediation* (pp. 447-482). New York: The Guildford Press; see also Kressel, K. (2014). The mediation of conflict: Context, cognition, and practice. In P. T. Coleman, M. Deutsch, & E. C. Marcus (pp. 817-848), *The handbook of conflict resolution: Theory and practice*. San Francisco, CA: Jossey-Bass.

2   See Malizia, D. A. & Jameson, J. K. (2018). Hidden in plain view: The impact of mediation on the mediator and implications for conflict resolution education. *Conflict Resolution Quarterly, 35*, 301-318; see also Lundberg, D. & Moloney, L. (2010). Being in the room: Family dispute resolution practitioners' experience of high conflict family dispute resolution. *Journal of Family Studies, 16*(3), 209-223.

3   See McDermott, E. P. (2012). Discovering the importance of mediator approach—An interdisciplinary challenge. *Negotiation and Conflict Management Research, 5*(4), 340-35; see also Lowry, L. R. (2004). Evaluative mediation. In J. Folberg, A. L. Milne, & P. Salem (Eds.), *Divorce and family mediation* (pp. 72-91). New York: The Guildford Press.

4   Waldman, E. (1996). The challenge of certification: How to ensure mediator competence while preserving diversity. *University of San Francisco Law Review, 30*, 723-1281.

5   See Winslade, J. (2006). Mediation with a focus on discursive positioning. *Conflict Resolution Quarterly, 23*(4), 501-515.

6   See, e.g., Friedman, G. & Himmelstein, J. (2008). *Challenging conflict: Mediation through understanding.* Chicago, IL: American Bar Association.

7   See Bush, R. A. B., & Folger, J. P. (2005). *The promise of mediation: The transformative approach to conflict.* San Francisco, CA: Jossey-Bass. For a more detailed discussion of the emphasis on empowerment as the goal of the process, see Bush, R. A. B. (2010). Taking self-determination seriously: The centrality of empowerment in transformative mediation. In J. P. Folger, R. A. B. Bush, & D. J. Della Noce (Eds.), *Transformative Mediation: A Sourcebook* (pp. 51-72). (n.p.): Institute for the Study of Conflict Transformation, Inc.

8   See Bush, R. A. B. & Pope, S. G. (2002). Changing the quality of conflict interaction: The principles and practice of transformative mediation. *Pepperdine Dispute Resolution Law Journal, 3*(1), 67-96.

9   Indiana Judicial Branch (n.d.). Mediation/Alternative Dispute Resolution. Retrieved from https://www.in.gov/judiciary/selfservice/2360.htm

10 Virginia's Judicial System (n.d.). Mediation. Retrieved from http://www.courts.state.va.us/courtadmin/aoc/djs/programs/drs/mediation/home.html

11 American Arbitration Association, American Bar Association, and Association for Conflict Resolution (2005). Model standards of conduct for mediators. Retrieved from https://www.adr.org/sites/default/files/document_repository/AAA%20Mediators%20Model%20Standards%20of%20Conduct%2010.14.2010.pdf

12 See Simon, D. (2012). Mediation redefined [blog post]. Retrieved from http://www.transformativemediation.org/mediation-redefined

13 See Charkoudian, L. (2012). Just my approach: The practical, ethical, and empirical dangers of the lack of

consensus about definitions of mediation approaches. *Negotiation and Conflict Management Research, 5*(4), 367-383; see also Wall, J. A., Dunne, T. C., & Chan-Serafin, S. (2011). The effects of neutral, evaluative, and pressing mediator strategies. *Conflict Resolution Quarterly, 29*(2), 127-150; Waldman, E. (1996). The challenge of certification: How to ensure mediator competence while preserving diversity. *University of San Francisco Law Review, 30*, 723-1281.

14   Kressel, K. & Wall, J. (2012). Introduction to the special issue on mediator approach. *Negotiation and Conflict Management Research, 5*(4), 334-339, at p. 336.

15   See Charkoudian (2012),.

16   Bush & Folger (2005).

17   See Riskin, L. L. (1996). Understanding mediator orientations, strategies and techniques: A grid for the perplexed. *Harvard Negotiation Law Review, 1*(38), 1–51; see also Riskin, L. L. (2003). Decision-making in mediation: The new old grid and the new grid system. *Notre Dame Law Review, 79*(1), 1-53.

18   Friedman & Himmelstein (2008).

19   Winslade, J. & Monk, G. (2001). *Narrative Mediation: A new approach to conflict resolution.* San Francisco, CA: Jossey-Bass.

2. EVALUATIVE MEDIATION

Evaluative mediation has two distinct, but overlapping, meanings (hence, I hereby declare it an approach and a half). I refer to these two versions of evaluative mediators as the *Dealmakers* and the *Judges*.

If you've ever seen mediation portrayed in a tv show or movie, you've probably seen the Dealmakers in action. Think of Vince Vaughn and Owen Wilson in the first scene of *Wedding Crashers,* saying whatever they can think of to get the couple to yes. When discussing how to divide the couple's frequent flyer miles, Jeremy (Vaughn) says, "This is just semantics, you guys wanna throw a couple miles at us, we'll take a couple. The big thing is that we're all moving on."[1] If you're a Dealmaker, you may have something in mind you think the parties will agree to if you present it the right way, but once they say yes, regardless of what they say yes to, your work is done.

This is how mediation is portrayed in popular culture, and for good reason. Many mediators practice this way, and, while those who've been trained differently might consider it "old school mediation,"[2] to many Dealmakers, it's just mediation.[3]

THE DEALMAKERS' THEORY AND GOALS

For the Dealmakers, the agreement is the main goal and top priority. In fact, when asked who their client is, these mediators may say that their client is "the deal."[4] Dealmakers seem to believe that the reason they were hired was to get the parties to an agreement, and in many cases they'd be right, even if that's only what the parties' lawyers wanted.[5] In addition to putting pressure on the other side, to some lawyers, it's the mediator's job to press the lawyer's *own* clients! These lawyers would prefer that the mediator be the one to break the bad news to the client – namely, that they might not win.[6]

Although self-serving motivations, such as gaining referrals from lawyers, could play a role in a mediator's decision to practice this way, most surely believe they're doing the parties a favor. After all, reaching a settlement can save people time, money, and the stress of a drawn-out court battle.[7] As *Wedding Crashers'* mediator, Jeremy, says to the divorcing wife's lawyer, "You know what, Ken? The bad idea would be to let your client walk out of here today and drag this thing out for another year, wasting more time and wasting more money."[8]

HOW DO THE DEALMAKERS DO IT?

With the agreement as the top priority, the Dealmakers will use (almost) any means (they deem) necessary to accomplish that goal. In fact, the Dealmakers in *Wedding Crashers* used some facilitative strategies, which we'll discuss later. However, as you might imagine, one of the main tools used by an evaluative mediator will be evaluations, and these are used selectively and strategically by the Dealmaker.

Share selective evaluations of each party's case

Dealmakers use evaluations in service of their ultimate goal, which is to get the parties to an agreement. So they do not share *all* evaluations with the parties; instead, the Dealmaker evaluates selectively. They get a sense of each side's case so they can emphasize, to each party, the weaknesses of their own position and strengths of the other's.[9] They try to convince both sides that they would be better off compromising.

Caucus

So now you may be asking yourself, *Won't each party hear the reasons that the other party's position is weak, making them even more attached to their own?* Good question. That could certainly happen if these conversations were happening with the parties together in the same room. This is where the *caucus* comes in. A caucus is when the mediator meets with each party, or side, separately. Mediators of other approaches may also caucus, for different reasons,[10] but the Dealmaker is mainly trying to manage the information each party hears.

As you might imagine, the Dealmaker is not saying the same things to each side when caucusing. In fact, some Dealmakers will intentionally mislead the parties about their assessment of the case, and about what the other party has said. The late John Cooley, a mediator, conflict resolution professor, and former United States Magistrate, made the somewhat shocking claim that deception is a necessary and commonly used tool in mediation. To be fair to Judge Cooley, you should know that he *did* call for clearer ethical standards around the use of what he affectionately referred to as the "noble lie."[11]

Mediator Jeff Kichaven, on the other hand, warns lawyers away from hiring mediators who use deception as part of their practice. Kichaven says that hiring a mediator to lie to your client is akin to you, the attorney, lying to your client, and is therefore grounds for disbarment.[12] This is no small claim since it takes *a lot* to get an attorney disbarred.[13]

Although Dealmakers generally apply pressure to both sides, they might not press both sides equally. That is, some Dealmakers apply more pressure to the side that they view as weaker, or more likely to move toward the other side's position, as a way of getting the parties to an agreement.[14]

Anything and everything

As mentioned earlier, the Dealmaker's primary, if not exclusive, goal is the agreement, and evaluation is just one strategy they use to achieve that goal. Over time, the term "evaluative" has essentially become synonymous with "directive," and is used to describe mediators who freely offer information, advice, and direction to the parties, whether or not legal evaluations are part of their toolkit.[15]

For example, a Dealmaker might rely on the age-old solution of suggesting the parties compromise or meet in the middle. In *Wedding Crashers*, as soon as the husband began to protest his wife's attempt to claim the frequent flyer miles, John (Wilson) said, "Ya know what we're gonna do? We're gonna split 'em right down the middle."[15]

And when things really seemed to be getting out of hand for the *Wedding Crashers*' parties, John tried to change the mood in the room by reminding the divorcing couple of good times they shared with each other: "You didn't always hate each other. There had to be some nice moments during the courtship maybe, or the wedding?"[16] Both mediators then waxed poetic about crab cakes and wedding bands, culminating in a brief rendition of The Isley Brothers' *Shout*. I'm not suggesting you try this yourself.

So Dealmakers are doing everything possible to get the parties to agree, regardless of what they agree to. However, the term *evaluative* is also used to describe mediators who slow the process down, sometimes deliberately moving parties *away* from an agreement. I call these mediators *Judges*, for reasons that will soon be clear.

THE JUDGES' THEORY AND GOALS

For the Judges, the goal of mediation is not to get the parties to just any agreement but rather to get them to the "right" agreement. This can mean steering the parties away from the "wrong" agreement, even if both are ready to say yes.

So the mediator still uses evaluations, but rather than looking at the strengths and weaknesses of each side's case, the *Judge* evaluates the parties' decisions, or the agreement as a whole. The mediator wants to make sure the decisions are good (or good *enough*), in the mediator's eyes.[17]

So what does a good enough decision look like? What yardstick will the mediator use? As you might imagine, it depends on the mediator. They might ask themselves, Is the agreement fair? Is it workable? Does it meet the parties' important needs? Does it meet the needs of any affected third parties, such as a divorcing couple's children? Does it line up, more or less, with what a court might order?

The mediator might also evaluate the *process* that led to the agreement: Were the decisions informed?

Were they made freely and voluntarily, or was one party pressured into the agreement by the other? And, of course, even mediators who ask the same questions may have different answers in terms of whether the agreement is fair *enough* or whether the process was voluntary *enough*.

The *Judge* is using evaluations to protect at least one of the parties, or a third party, from a harmful or unfair outcome.[18] They may also be trying to protect the agreement from being challenged or overturned later. The mediator wants to make sure the agreement is durable – that everyone involved will be okay with it once the dust settles, and that any (actual) judge who might evaluate it in the future will not find anything too concerning. Any or all of these reasons could motivate the mediator to nudge the parties toward one outcome and away from another.

HOW DO THE JUDGES DO IT?

With the goal of helping the parties reach the "right" agreement, or at least avoid the "wrong" agreement, *Judges* will guide the process – some more directly and transparently than others.

Straight up, tell the parties what they should do

Some Judge-style evaluative mediators share their evaluations early in the process and urge the parties to follow them.[19] After gathering information the mediator sees as relevant, they will share their assessment of where the parties should land, which is usually based on legal statutes or precedent.

In a divorce case, the mediator might ask the parties about their incomes and parenting schedule. The mediator would then apply any child support or spousal support formulas to the information from the parties and tell them that this is what a judge would likely order. The mediator would use these calculations to suggest (explicitly or implicitly) that the parties settle on these amounts.

The same strategy might also be used by the Dealmaker, but for a different reason. The Dealmaker would view this strategy as an efficient way to get the parties to an agreement, while the Judge would perform these calculations to lead the parties to the "correct" agreement. The Dealmaker and Judge also differ in how they would respond if the parties decided to deviate from the formulas; the Dealmaker would have no objection as long as the parties were agreeing to *something*, while the Judge's response would depend on what the parties were agreeing to, and why.

A smorgasbord of practices, unless and until the mediator sees a problem

Instead of sharing their evaluations at the beginning of the process, with the goal of leading the parties to the "right" agreement, some Judge-style mediators would begin by using any number of practices we'll be covering in this book, and only share their evaluation if the parties seemed to be narrowing in on the "wrong" agreement – one that was far afield from what the mediator thought was fair or reasonable.[20] At that point, the mediator would raise their concerns, either directly or indirectly.

Reality testing - hypothetical situations

An *indirect* way that a mediator may raise their concerns is by asking the parties questions designed to expose possible flaws in the parties' plan, also known as *reality testing*.[21] For example, if a divorcing couple agreed that the wife will keep the marital home, the mediator might ask how the parties will afford the mortgage payments if the wife's new business does not take off as quickly as she anticipates. Following this line of questioning, the parties may change their plan, or perhaps build in some safeguards. At least, that would be the mediator's hope.

Reality testing - current practical and legal information

The mediator might also reality test more directly, for instance, by asking the parties to take a closer look at their budgets to see if their income and expenses lined up. And if the clients (or their attorneys) seem to be mistaken about relevant laws, the mediator might suggest a look-see.[22]

Share the evaluation directly
Some mediators will simply tell the parties there is a fatal flaw in the agreement they are considering. The mediator would inform the parties that their decisions are illegal or unconscionable, or for other reasons would be unacceptable to a court. [23]

Withdraw
If the parties are determined to make a decision that troubles the mediator *enough*, the mediator may decide to withdraw from the case. Mediators draw lines in different places, of course, and for different reasons. Gary Friedman, an understanding-based mediator (an approach we'll be covering in Chapter 5), will withdraw if the parties insist on an agreement that "a court would deem illegal," or one that is "so unfair that [he] could not, in good conscience, write it up."[24] As mentioned earlier, some mediators will also consider the *way* the decisions were made, and withdraw if the agreement appeared to be motivated by "ignorance, coercion, or duress."[25]

As you've seen, the *Judge* version of evaluative mediation covers a range of practices, and many mediators who use these practices would probably not consider themselves evaluative at all. The narrower the range of decisions accepted by the mediator, and the more directive the mediator is (i.e., sharing their evaluations and recommendations relatively early in the process while urging the parties to follow them), the more likely it is that the mediator would be considered evaluative by their peers (and perhaps themselves).

In contrast, mediators who accept a broader range of options, and offer evaluations only when things seem to be going awry, would likely label their approach another way.[26] These mediators would still be called "evaluative" by mediators who are less likely to evaluate in the same situation. On the other hand, those who *do* evaluate in a given situation might question the judgment (and ethics) of those who do not. As an observant comedian once quipped, "Have you ever noticed that anybody driving slower than you is an idiot, and anyone going faster than you is a maniac?"[27] Same thing.

IRONIES AND EXPLANATIONS OF EVALUATIVE MEDIATION

Somewhat ironically, mediators can be called evaluative when they seem to be doing everything possible to get the parties to agree, regardless of what they agree to (the *Dealmakers*), and they can be called evaluative when they try to slow the parties down and move them away from an agreement they seem to be heading toward (the *Judges*).

These different forms of evaluative mediation tend to show up differently in different cases. Despite what we observed in *Wedding Crashers*, the *Dealmaker* is likely to find a home in commercial cases, whereas the *Judge* is more likely to find a home in family or divorce cases.[28]

Why might this be?

In commercial cases, the parties are generally represented by lawyers, and are often repeat players. With all of that legal sophistication in the room, the mediator will feel less of a need to protect the parties.[29] To the mediator, it's the lawyer's job to protect their client, and the mediator's job to get the parties to an agreement. Also, the lawyers may be hiring the mediator precisely because the mediator has a reputation for getting results (i.e., settlements), so the mediator will be even more motivated to continue to do so, whatever it takes.

In contrast, people divorcing are often going through the process for the first time, generally without lawyers. When lawyers are involved, they're more likely to serve as consultants outside of the sessions than participate in the mediation itself. Without lawyers in the room advocating for their clients, the mediator may feel the need to think of objections the parties' lawyers (real or hypothetical) would have to the agreement.

Also, decisions made during a divorce often directly affect children, whom the mediator may feel obliged to protect.[30] For similar reasons, the Judge-style approach is also likely to find a home in other cases directly affecting third parties, such as environmental and bioethical (e.g., involving the termination of life support) disputes.[31]

And unlike commercial cases, where win-lose options are common in litigation (e.g., either liability is established or it is not, there was a breach of contract or there was not), in family mediations, the questions and answers are more nuanced: How much child support is the right amount? How should the assets be divided? How should parenting time be arranged? In these cases, Judge-style evaluative mediators often think that they have a sense of what a judge would do (and they may, as evaluative mediators of both types are often retired judges[32]), so an evaluative mediator of the Judge variety may attempt to lead the parties toward such an outcome, or simply dissuade them from an outcome that seems too far outside the norm.

Finally, many divorcing couples hire their attorney-mediators to draft the settlement agreement following mediation. This additional role adds a layer of responsibility to the role of the mediator because an attorney cannot draft a contract they know to be illegal.[33] So mediators who are also planning to draft the parties' agreement may feel they need to steer people away from decisions they would be unwilling to draft.

You could view the *Judge* and the *Dealmaker* as two ends of a continuum when it comes to concern with the content of the parties' agreement. However, many evaluative mediators practice a blend of these two approaches – they strategically share evaluations to help the parties reach an agreement, while also evaluating and maintaining standards for the agreement.

Mediators who practice this way are probably the most likely to use the term "evaluative mediation" (as opposed to simply calling it "mediation") to describe what they do.[34]

As mentioned earlier, evaluative mediation is often practiced by retired judges; in that role, they likely witnessed the extensive financial and emotional costs of court firsthand, and became convinced that there had to be a better way. Whether closer to the *Dealmaker* or *Judge* variety, they bring familiar aspects of the court to their role as a mediator, including a focus on legal precedent and comfort with at least *some* degree of direction from a neutral third party.

Many mediators practicing other approaches acknowledge that evaluative mediation (of either variety) may serve a purpose, and may be exactly what some parties want. However, these mediators argue that the evaluative approach is more akin to other alternative dispute resolution processes, such as settlement conferencing or early neutral evaluation, and, for clarity's sake, should not be called mediation.[35]

So that's the evaluative approach in a nutshell. Now let's move on to the approach that is often contrasted with both versions of the evaluative approach, facilitative mediation.

1   Abrams, P. Levy, R.L., Panay, A. (Producers), & Dobkin, D. (Director). (2005). *Wedding Crashers* [Motion Picture]. United States: New Line Cinema.

2   Simon, D. (n.d.). Old-school mediation techniques [blog post]. Retrieved from https://transformativemediation.com/old-school-mediation/

3   Charkoudian, L., De Ritis, C., Buck, R., & Wilson, C. L. (2009). Mediation by any other name would smell as sweet—or would it? The struggle to define mediation and its various approaches. *Conflict Resolution Quarterly, 26*(3), 293-316, at pp. 310-11 (noting that none of the mediators in their sample identified their approach as "evaluative," even though they endorsed evaluative goals and strategies [and many did not label their approach at all]).

4   See Kichaven, J. (2011). Use a mediator, get disbarred. Retrieved from https://jeffkichaven.com/wp-content/uploads/2017/10/GetDisbarredWebsite.pdf

5   See Raines, S. S., Pokhrel, S. K., & Poitras, J. (2013). Mediation as a profession: Challenges that professional mediators face. *Conflict Resolution Quarterly, 21*(1), 79-97

6   See Bickerman, J. (1996). Evaluative mediator responds. *Alternatives to the High Cost of Litigation, 14*(6), 70; see also Lowry, L. R. (2004). Evaluative mediation. In J. Folberg, A. L. Milne, & P. Salem (Eds.), *Divorce and family mediation* (pp. 72-91). New York: The Guildford Press.

7   See Lowry (2004).

8   Abrams et al. (2005).

9   If you're considering practicing this way, please note that ethical issues may be implicated when providing

legal evaluations, or anything that could be construed as legal advice (as opposed to legal information), in the context of mediation, particularly when the mediator is not an attorney. See Welsh, N. (2001). The thinning vision of self-determination in court-connected mediation: The inevitable price of institutionalization? *Harvard Negotiation Law Review, 6*(1), 27-96, at p. 50, n. 211; see also American Bar Association Section of Dispute Resolution (2002). Mediation and the unauthorized practice of law. Retrieved from https://www.mediate.com/articles/abaupl.cfm; see also Currie, C. (2000). Should a mediator also be an attorney? Retrieved from https://www.mediate.com/articles/currie.cfm

10 Mediators practicing other approaches also use caucuses, but for different reasons (e.g., to help a party achieve clarity about their own goals, preferences, and options); Institute for the Study of Conflict Transformation, Inc. (2010). *Mediation: Principles & practice, the transformative approach* [training manual].

11 Cooley, J. (2000). Defining the ethical limits of acceptable deception in mediation, The Problem section, para. 7. Retrieved from https://www.mediate.com/articles/cooley1.cfm

12 Kichaven (2011).

13 See Sinberg, S. (2014). Getting disbarred is harder than you think [blog post]. Retrieved from https://www.rocketlawyer.com/blog/getting-disbarred-is-harder-than-you-think-915832

14 McDermott, E. P. (2012). Discovering the importance of mediator approach—An interdisciplinary challenge. *Negotiation and Conflict Management Research, 5*(4), 340-353, at p. 341-42 (Patrick McDermott shares his experiences

with mediators in the Equal Employment Opportunity Commission context who seemed to "beat down" the side perceived as weaker, which was often the plaintiff).

15   See Charkoudian et al. (2009), at p. 311.

16   Abrams et al. (2005).

17   Abrams et al. (2005).

18   See Waldman, E. (2011). *Mediation ethics: Cases and commentaries.* San Francisco, CA: Jossey-Bass, at p. 21.

19   See Waldman, E. (1996). The challenge of certification: How to ensure mediator competence while preserving diversity. *University of San Francisco Law Review, 30,* 723-1281, at pp. 741-742.

20   Riskin, L. (1994). Mediator orientations, strategies and techniques. *Alternatives to the High Cost of Litigation, 12*(9), 111-14, at p. 114.

21   Nolan-Haley, J. (2011). Comments on cases 5.3 and 5.4. In E. Waldman (Ed.), *Mediation ethics: Cases and commentaries* (pp. 146-151). San Francisco, CA: Jossey-Bass, at pp. 149-150.

22   See Charkoudian, L. (2012). Just my approach: The practical, ethical, and empirical dangers of the lack of consensus about definitions of mediation approaches. *Negotiation and Conflict Management Research, 5*(4), 367-383, at pp. 369-370 (discussing the different potential meanings of "reality testing").

23   Nolan-Haley (2011), at p. 150.

24   See Waldman (1996), at pp. 740-742.

25 Friedman, G. J. (1993). *A guide to divorce mediation: How to reach a fair, legal settlement at a fraction of the cost*. New York, NY: Workman Publishing, at p. 30.

26 Waldman (1996), at p. 741.

27 See Lowry (2004), at p. 84; see also Welsh, N. (2001). The thinning vision of self-determination in court-connected mediation: The inevitable price of institutionalization? *Harvard Negotiation Law Review, 6*(1), 27-32, at p. 5.

28 George Carlin Quotes. (n.d.). BrainyQuote.com. Retrieved August 9, 2019, from BrainyQuote.com Web site: https://www.brainyquote.com/quotes/george_carlin_391403

29 In a brief introduction to L. Randolph Lowry's chapter on evaluative mediation (Lowry, 2004), the book's editors (Folberg, Milne, & Salem) note that evaluative mediation is common in commercial cases, and more controversial in divorce cases (p. 72). However, their use of the term, "evaluative," does not differentiate between the two versions of evaluative mediation described herein. The second version of evaluative mediation described here (the *Judges*) corresponds to the approach that Ellen Waldman (1996), terms "norm-advocating," and she notes that this approach is often used in divorce cases (p. 741).

30 See Wall, J. A. & Dunne, T. C. (2012). Mediation research: A current review. *Negotiation Journal, 28*(2), 217-244, at pp. 220-221.

31 The Model Standards of Practice for Family and Divorce Mediation (Symposium on Standards of Practice for Family and Divorce Mediation Convened by the Association of Family and Conciliation Courts, 2000. *Model standards of practice for family and divorce mediation*. Retrieved from https://www.afccnet.org/Portals/0/PublicDocuments/

CEFCP/ModelStandardsOfPracticeForFamilyAndDivorceMediation.pdf), which direct the mediator to "assist parties in determining how to promote the best interests of children" (Standard VIII), may also play a role in the family mediator's use of evaluation for protective purposes. Given the apparent inconsistencies within and between standards promulgated by mediation organizations and regulatory bodies, a discussion of the standards is beyond the scope of this book. See Bush, R. A. B. (2019). A pluralistic approach to mediation ethics: Delivering on mediation's different promises. *Ohio State Journal on Dispute Resolution, 34*(3), 459-535; see also Exon, S. N. (2006). How can a mediator be both impartial and fair: Why ethical standards of conduct create chaos for mediators. *Journal of Dispute Resolution, 2006*(2), 387-434; see also Waldman (2011), at pp. 11-14.

32 See Waldman (1996).

33 Milne, A. L., Folberg, J. & Salem, P. (2004). The evolution of divorce and family mediation. In J. Folberg, A. L. Milne, & P. Salem (Eds.), *Divorce and family mediation* (pp. 72-91). New York: The Guildford Press.

34 See Welsh (2001).

35 See Lowry (2004); Bickerman (1996).

36 E.g., Bertz, C., & Erickson, S. K. (2013, Winter). Response to Larry Gaughan's article. *The Professional Family Mediator*, pp. 4, 10. Retrieved from https://apfmnet.org/wp-content/uploads/APFM-newsletter-2013-Winter.pdf

3. FACILITATIVE MEDIATION

If you've spent any time in the world of mediation, you've probably at least heard the term *facilitative mediation*, as that is probably the most common label that mediators use to describe what they do, if they use a label at all.[1] Like evaluative mediation, there are no specific founders of facilitative mediation, so nowhere to find an exact definition, or a definitive theoretical basis for the approach.[2]

THEORY AND GOALS

Although people often contrast facilitative mediation with evaluative mediation,[3] the approaches share a primary goal, which is to help the parties reach an agreement.[4] John Haynes, an early leader in the facilitative approach, described the mediator's role as the "manager of negotiations."[5]

Unlike evaluative mediators, facilitative mediators believe the parties should control the terms of the agreement. The facilitative mediator wants to help the parties put the conflict behind them as quickly and efficiently as possible, but they also want the parties to reach an agreement that they've chosen, preferably one that meets everyone's needs as well as possible.[6]

Also unlike evaluative mediators, who largely rely on legal precedent to shape parties' outcomes, facilitative mediators (who could be retired judges or lawyers, but are also likely to come from mental health backgrounds) believe that parties are capable of reaching *better* agreements than a judge or lawyer could craft for them.[7] Facilitative mediators believe that, when people work together and collaborate rather than compete, they can think outside the box and find solutions that work well for everyone.

HOW DO THEY DO IT?

In contrast to the Dealmakers, who stress the weaknesses of each party's case to motivate them to settle, the facilitative mediator does not *primarily* rely on the parties' fear of loss as a motivator. They might stress the emotional and financial costs of a court battle, especially if the parties seemed to be at an impasse. However, the facilitative mediator largely focuses on the parties' hopes or desires, encouraging them to collaborate with each other to get everyone's needs met.[8]

Establishing ground Rules

Facilitative mediators sometimes begin a mediation by discussing ground rules for the parties, which often involve the way the parties communicate with each other. Ground rules may also set expectations for other aspects of the process, such as how the parties prepare for sessions and share information.[9] The mediator might be the one to set the rules, or they may just suggest rules for the parties to adopt, such as:

> We agree to take turns speaking and to try to not interrupt each other…We agree to call each other by our first names, not 'he' or 'she' or worse… We agree to make a conscious, sincere effort to refrain from unproductive arguing, venting, and narration and agree to use our time in mediation to work toward what we perceive to be our most constructive agreement possible.[10]

Facilitative mediators are also likely to enforce the rules, at least when they believe the rule violation is causing a problem.[11]

Normalizing

Facilitative mediators frequently suggest that the parties' problems are "normal" problems. Normal problems are presumably solvable problems since others have solved them before.[12] So if a father says his children have a good time when they're with him, while the mother says they cry when it's time to go to

Dad's, the facilitative mediator might respond in the following way:

> It's not unusual for them, by the way, to have this tension and lots of crying when they go back and when they come forward and some apprehension. Obviously they're still trying to sort out how to behave in relationship to each of you, when you're living apart as distinct from when you were living together. So it is perfectly possible for them to have a good time when with you, Michael, but also express real concerns and reservations when they're with you, Debra. That's not an unusual situation.[13]

Reframing

Facilitative mediators try to keep the tone of the conversation positive, or at least neutral.[14] So when a husband yells, *My wife always puts me down in front of the kids! I hate it when she does that!* the mediator might reframe this by saying, *You'd like your wife to speak to you in a respectful way when the kids are around.* The mediator deliberately took something that had been phrased in a negative way (what the husband hates), removed the hostile tone and language, and framed it as a wish or preference (what the husband would like to see going forward).

Emphasizing common ground

Facilitative mediators often try to find and emphasize common ground, or areas of agreement, between the parties.[15] This comes up in parenting, where the parties may disagree about a number of things, but still have a shared love for their children. To establish common ground, the mediator might follow a heated conversation about parenting decisions with the statement, *It's clear that you both care deeply for your children and want the best for them.* In *Wedding Crashers*, the mediators used marriage itself as a common enemy to unite the couple when Jeremy (Vince Vaughn) said, "Guys, the real enemy here is the institution of marriage. It's not realistic. It's crazy!"[16]

Mutualizing

Mutualizing is kind of like emphasizing common ground, but it focuses on the parties' shared responsibility for the problem.[17] So if both parties are complaining about the other failing to listen, the mediator might say, "I assume you both want to be heard."[18] As *Wedding Crashers'* John (Owen Wilson) suggested to the divorcing couple, "All we're trying to say is, put your swords away for a second."[19] The idea is that a mutual problem requires a mutual solution and everyone's efforts.

Focusing on the future

As you might imagine, mediators focused on the goal of getting the parties to an agreement will direct parties away from discussions about the past, and point them toward the future. So if the parties are talking about the reasons that they're getting divorced, or complaining about the other person's past bad behavior, a facilitative mediator might say, *There's nothing that can be done about what happened in the past, and you're probably always going to see it a little bit differently. It might be more helpful, instead, to think about what you want your futures to look like so you can move forward.*

Or in the words of *Wedding Crashers'* Jeremy, "Hey, don't do this for the other person. It's about saying yes to yourself and saying yes to your future."[20]

Interest-based problem-solving

The meat of the facilitative approach can be found in the methods they use to expand the range of possible solutions to the parties' problem. Instead of encouraging clients to compromise or meet in the middle, as the Dealmaker might, they try to shift the conversation away from the parties' *positions* and toward their *interests*.[21]

And what do I mean by "positions" and "interests"? *Positions* are usually what the parties come in saying they want. For example, they may say that they want the house and full custody of the children. Often the parties' positions are narrow and incompatible – they can't both have exclusive use of the house, or full custody of the children.

But if you look at the parties' *interests*, or *why* they want what they want, you may find that these are compatible with each other. So an *interest* would be the need, or want, that a *position* is designed to meet. In this case, the parties both might *actually* just want a comfortable living situation in a convenient location, along with substantial quality time with the children – interests that are not necessarily incompatible. The assumption is that if people focus less on their narrow positions, and more on their broader interests, they'll be able to find solutions that will satisfy everyone.

An example can be found in *Getting to Yes*,[22] a classic text on methods of negotiation. In this book, the authors describe a situation where two children are fighting over an orange. Each of their positions is, *I should have the orange*. Clearly, their positions are incompatible, although their interests might not be.

So if you wanted to understand the children's interests, you would find out *why* they each wanted the orange. In this example, one child wants to make juice out of the pulp, and the other wants to use the peel to make a zest for a cake. Conveniently, their interests are completely compatible - one can have the peel and the other can have the pulp, and neither gives up anything important to them.

It doesn't always work out that perfectly in the real world, of course, but a more realistic example might come up when a divorcing couple is trying to divide their assets. The facilitative mediator would focus less on trying to determine what kind of distribution was fair, or what a court might order (areas where an evaluative mediator might focus the discussion), and would instead focus on the parties' interests, recognizing that some assets may be more valuable to one party than the other.

In this example, the wife might want to go back to school so that she can get a job with more earning potential, whereas the husband might be content with his career and current income but concerned about having enough when he retires. Here, the wife would benefit from liquid assets she could use right away, whereas the husband would benefit from assets that were likely to appreciate over time. In this case, the parties' interests are more compatible than their positions would have been had they focused only on their account balances.

So the facilitative mediator uses future-focused, interest-based discussions to expand the pie, allowing each party to walk away with more than they would if they focused solely on their positions. The mediator encourages the parties to focus on *why* they want what they want, with the hope that they can then increase their pool of options and find solutions that work well for everyone.

THEORY AND GOALS, REVISITED

Normally when people talk about facilitative mediation, they have in mind a way of mediating that is different from both definitions of evaluative mediation that we covered. Rather than trying to get the parties to an agreement by any means necessary, facilitative mediators at least *begin* by doing what they can to put the parties in a positive frame of mind. They encourage the parties to focus on *why* they want what they want, and to collaborate with each other so that everyone can get their important needs met. However, some facilitative mediators will resort to fear-based pressure tactics (generally by focusing on the costs and risks of litigation) if the positive approach doesn't seem to be working (i.e., the parties seem far from an agreement).

And rather than trying to move the parties toward a "good" agreement or away from a "bad" one, the facilitative mediator usually assumes that, by encouraging the parties to collaborate and focus on their interests, they will come to an agreement that satisfies them both. For this reason, and because reaching an agreement is the primary goal of the facilitative approach, the mediator generally refrains from evaluating the parties' joint decisions.[23]

And now, for the next stop on our tour of mediation approaches – the last of the "Big Three" – we have another approach you've probably heard of, and that's transformative mediation.

1   Charkoudian, L. (2012). Just my approach: The practical, ethical, and empirical dangers of the lack of consensus about definitions of mediation approaches. *Negotiation and Conflict Management Research, 5*(4), 367-383.

2   See Mayer, B. (2004). Facilitative mediation. In J. Folberg, A. L. Milne, & P. Salem (Eds.), *Divorce and family mediation* (pp. 29-52). New York: The Guildford Press.

3   Wall, J. A. & Kressel, K. (2012). Research on mediator approach: A summary and some research suggestions. *Negotiation and Conflict Management Research, 5*(4), 403-421, at p. 414.

4   See Bingham, L. B. (2012). Transformative mediation at the United States Postal Service. *Negotiation and Conflict Management Research, 5*(4), 354-366; See also Simon, D. (2010). Transformative mediation for divorce: Rising above the law and the settlement. In J. P. Folger, R. A. B. Bush, & D. J. Della Noce (Eds.), *Transformative Mediation: A Sourcebook* (pp. 249-270). (n.p.): Institute for the Study of Conflict Transformation, Inc.

5   Haynes, J. M. (1994). *The fundamentals of family mediation.* Albany: State University of New York Press, at p. 15.

6   See Love, L. (2011). Comments on cases 5.3 and 5.4. In E. Waldman (Ed.), *Mediation ethics: Cases and commentaries* (pp. 136-146). San Francisco, CA: Jossey-Bass.

7   See Mayer (2004); see also Riskin, L. (1994). Mediator orientations, strategies and techniques. *Alternatives to the High Cost of Litigation, 12*(9), 111–14; Waldman, E. (2011). *Mediation ethics: Cases and commentaries.* San Francisco, CA: Jossey-Bass.

8   See Bingham (2012), at pp. 357-58; See Mayer (2004), at p. 44.

9   See Haynes (1994), at pp. 46-47.

10 Melamed, J. (2018). Sample mediation ground rules, para. 4. Retrieved from https://www.mediate.com/articles/melamed7.cfm

11 See Haynes (1994), at p. 47.

12 See Haynes (1994), at p. 9.

13 Haynes (1994), at p. 10.

14 See Charkoudian (2012); see also Mayer (2004).

15 See Charkoudian (2012).

16 Abrams, P. Levy, R.L., Panay, A. (Producers), & Dobkin, D. (Director). (2005). *Wedding Crashers* [Motion Picture]. United States: New Line Cinema, scene 1.

17 See Haynes (1994).

18 Haynes (1994), at p. 11.

19 Abrams et al. (2005).

20 Abrams et al. (2005).

21 See Mayer (2004).

22 Fisher, W., Ury, R. & Patton, B. (2011). *Getting to yes: Negotiating agreement without giving in.* New York, NY: Penguin Books.

23 See Mayer (2004), at pp. 39-40.

4. TRANSFORMATIVE MEDIATION

Unlike both the facilitative and evaluative approaches, transformative mediation is a mediation *model*. It has an explicit theoretical basis and clearly defined practices, which Baruch Bush and Joseph Folger describe in *The Promise of Mediation: The Transformative Approach to Conflict*.[1] Therefore, mediators who are truly practicing transformative mediation will likely be more similar to each other in the way they practice than would two randomly chosen facilitative or evaluative mediators.[2]

THEORY AND GOALS

So, what is transformative mediation, and how does it differ from the facilitative and evaluative approaches? Transformative mediation is based on a specific theory of conflict – what conflict looks like, what keeps us stuck there, and how we can find our way through it. This theory of conflict is based on research from several different areas, including communication theory, social psychology, political science, and moral philosophy.[3] The basic idea is that, in a state of conflict, we tend to experience both *weakness* (meaning, we're confused and scared) and *self-absorption* (meaning, we can only see things from our own perspective), in relation to each other.

Wait. People can be weak and self-absorbed at the same time? Isn't this a contradiction? You might think that people who feel weak aren't thinking of themselves at all – they're just doing what the other person wants and prioritizing the other person's needs. And you might think that people who are self-absorbed feel strong – they're taking care of their own needs rather than worrying about anyone else. However, according to the transformative theory, when people are in conflict, these states of weakness and self-absorption often go together. Allow me to explain.

In a state of weakness, we feel overwhelmed by the situation and unsure how to handle it. We don't feel confident in our ability to do what we need to do, or even *know* what we need to do. We feel like we're under threat and need to protect ourselves. In this state, there's no room to let the other person's viewpoint in, so we can only see things from our own perspective – in other words, we're self-absorbed. That's how feeling weak can lead to self-absorption.

And when we're self-absorbed and seeing things only from our own perspective, it is difficult to see and understand the other person as a fellow human being. Instead, they are viewed as an obstacle or a threat. In this state, we might feel the urge to attack the other person to fend off the threat, but that urge is not coming from a place of strength; it's coming from desperation, or even panic. Alternatively, we might feel the urge to give in and let the person have whatever they want, but that's not because we can see things from the other person's point of view; it's because we want to make the threat go away.

And now our self-absorbed behavior toward the other person – whether we're attacking them or giving in – confuses us even more because that's not who we truly are; that's not how we treat others, or ourselves. This leads us to feel even weaker, and, consequently, more self-absorbed. So these states of weakness and self-absorption can reinforce each other within each person in the conflict.

These states can also reinforce each other *between* the people in conflict, creating a "vicious circle." It works like this: When I am trying to protect myself and am unable to see things from your perspective, I start treating you in a closed off way – more like an enemy than a fellow human. The more I treat you like an enemy, the weaker and more closed off *you* feel. You then treat *me* like an enemy, leading me to feel even weaker and more closed off to you, and so on. According to transformative theory, this is the vicious circle of conflict that people are desperate to escape.

But there's good news – the vicious circle of conflict can be reversed and become a "virtuous circle."[4] This virtuous circle, as you might imagine, occurs when people in conflict are becoming stronger (instead of weaker) and more responsive to each other (instead of self-absorbed). And these states are also self-perpetuating.

The virtuous circle reinforces itself *within* each person like this: The stronger and clearer I feel, the less I need to protect myself, and the more open I can be to your perspective. This allows me to feel more connected, and to behave in ways that I can feel good about. This makes me feel even stronger because I'm living up to my ideals. Even if I disagree with you, I can hear you without viewing or treating you like an enemy.

And this virtuous circle reinforces itself *between* people in the conflict like this: The more open and responsive I am to you, the clearer and stronger you feel, and the less you need to demonize me. This allows you to treat me in a more responsive, connected way, leading me to feel even stronger and more open to you, and so on. This is where the transformative theory assumes that people want to be.

Transformative theory is based on the idea that people value both their autonomy and their connections with others.[5] We don't want to hurt or victimize others; nor do we want to be victimized ourselves. We want to make choices and connect with others in a way that acknowledges our humanity, and theirs.

So now if you think back to some of your worst conflicts, where you felt trapped in that vicious circle, did you stay there forever? Probably not. In most cases, the conflict was resolved somehow – you were able to get to a place where you felt stronger and clearer about what you needed to do, and you were able to see the other person as a person again. Even if you decided to part ways, the hostility likely died down, and the other person lost their status as enemy.

According to transformative theory, you escaped the conflict trap by moving from the vicious circle, where you felt weak and self-absorbed, to the virtuous circle, where you felt strong and responsive. However, this probably did not happen all at once. Instead, it probably happened through small, subtle shifts, where you each grew stronger and more responsive to each other.

In transformative lingo, these shifts are known as *empowerment shifts* (you're becoming empowered as you shift in the direction from weakness to strength), and *recognition shifts* (you're recognizing the other person as a person as you shift in the direction from self-absorption to responsiveness). Transformative mediators view these shifts as indicators of a high-quality outcome. According to transformative theory, people in conflict *want* to make these empowerment and recognition shifts and are usually perfectly capable of doing so when they have the right support.[6]

So transformative mediators use practices that are designed to support the parties and put them in the best position to make those shifts. As such, the main goal of the transformative mediator is to participate in a high-quality process, which is defined by what the mediator does, rather than by what the parties do.

HOW DO THEY DO IT?

Transformative mediators support the parties using the practices of *reflection*, *summary*, and the *check-in*. But first, the mediator sets the stage with the opening statement.

The opening statement

Did I say first? I meant second. Before making an opening statement, the transformative mediator asks the parties if they would like to hear one. The mediator might ask, "Would you like me to say a few words about the process before we begin?" And then, only if the parties say yes, does the mediator describe how they see the process.

The mediator explains that their role is to support the parties in their conversation. The mediator might ask the parties if there is anything they need to help the conversation go as well as possible, but the mediator does not impose any rules or guidelines for the parties to follow. Unlike the facilitative mediator, who might establish or suggest ground rules for the parties, the transformative mediator puts the decisions about communication, information sharing, and all aspects of the process in the parties' hands.

The transformative mediator often says a few words about confidentiality (e.g., that the mediator will hold all that is said by the parties confidential), and leaves room for the parties to discuss any expectations or concerns they have about confidentiality, if they wish. The mediator also uses the opening statement to describe the practices the mediator will use, such as the practice of *reflection*.

Reflection

Reflection is when the mediator reflects, like a mirror, what the speaker said.[7] In the example used in our discussion of the facilitative approach, you'll recall that the husband yelled, *My wife always puts me down in front of the kids! I hate it when she does that!* In that situation, the facilitative mediator *reframed* the statement by turning down the volume and changing it from negative (what the husband hated) to positive (what he wanted).

The transformative mediator would instead *reflect* that statement back to the husband, as accurately as possible. The mediator might say, *You hate that! You hate it when your wife puts you down in front of the kids, and she always does that!* You'll notice that the mediator used many of the words the husband used.

In transformative mediation, mediators tend to believe that the parties are in the best position to know what words they meant to use, and why.

The transformative mediator tries to accurately capture what the party said, rather than reframe it, as a facilitative mediator would. Additionally, the transformative mediator reflects the energy or intensity conveyed by the speaker. So if the husband sounded emotional when he made the statement about his wife, the mediator would try to match the husband's energy when reflecting what the husband said.

Why might the mediator accurately reflect what the husband said, even if he used some hostile words, and even if he sounded angry when he did so? What is the mediator trying to accomplish? When the mediator accurately reflects what the husband said, including the energy behind his expression, the husband not only feels heard (emotion and all), but he is now able to hear himself. This gives him a chance to figure out if that *was* what he meant to say, and how he meant to say it.[8]

The husband can respond in any number of ways. For instance, he could confirm that, yes indeed, that was what he meant to say. The husband could say, *Yeah, I really do hate that!* Or he could expand on what he said by adding more, such as, *Yeah, and the kids don't like it either!* Or he could retract, clarify, or perhaps tone down, what he said. For example, he might say, *Well, I guess she doesn't always do that, but it just happened the other day and it really got to me.*

So the mediator's reflection provided an opportunity for the husband to hear his own words and clarify his own thoughts. According to transformative theory, the husband is making empowerment shifts as he's getting clearer; that is, he's moving from a place of weakness to strength.[9]

Putting what one party said back into the room by saying it again can also help the other party in the room (in this case, the wife) hear those words in a way she couldn't before. Sometimes when people are in conflict, they almost block each other's voices out – they simply can't hear each other anymore.[10] But when the mediator repeats what one party said (in this case, the husband), and those words are now in the mediator's voice rather than the husband's voice, the wife can more clearly hear the husband.

The husband is also likely speaking in a calmer, clearer way as he makes these empowerment shifts, which should further contribute to his wife's ability to hear and understand him.[11] And now, as the wife becomes more open to her husband, she's making recognition shifts – she's moving *away* from self-absorption and *toward* responsiveness. So a reflection provides an opportunity for both parties to make shifts away from the vicious circle and toward the virtuous circle.

The mediator reflects one person at a time, usually right after a party speaks. Of course, the mediator does not reflect *everything* each party says – that would be distracting, and would likely interfere with, rather than support, the parties' conversation. Instead, transformative mediators look for signals that a reflection would be helpful and supportive in that moment.

When a reflection would not be helpful, the mediator remains silent. In those moments, the mediator is still listening closely, and may bring each party's words back into the room a little bit later, in a different way. This brings us to the *summary*.

Summary

There might be times when there is either not much room or not much of a need for the mediator to reflect. During these interactions, the mediator pays close attention to the what the parties are saying, keeping track of their main points and perspectives on each topic they discuss.

Then, when there's a pause in the conversation, or whenever it seems like it would be helpful to do so, the mediator *summarizes* the conversation.[12] The mediator organizes the conversation according to themes, or topics, and summarizes them one at a time. The mediator notes the different perspectives that the parties shared, including where the parties seem to agree and where they seem to disagree. The mediator is careful not to shy away from intense emotions, strong disagreements, or topics that may not seem relevant from a problem-solving perspective. From a transformative mediator's perspective, the parties are the best judge of what they need to discuss, and how.

Summaries can be short and focused (e.g., covering what the parties just discussed over the previous few minutes), or longer and general (e.g., covering all the topics that were discussed throughout the session). Summaries can include topics and perspectives already reflected by the mediator in addition to those not yet reflected. According to the transformative model, hearing the conversation organized this way can help both parties get clearer on how they view each topic in relation to each other, and then figure out what they would like to do next. This brings us to the *check-in.*

Check-In

In addition to *reflecting* and *summarizing*, transformative mediators *check in* with the parties and provide an opportunity for each party to make decisions in the moment. For example, right after a summary, the mediator might ask the parties where they want to go from there.[13] The mediator might say, *Would you like to talk more about any of these topics? Or maybe there's something else you'd like to talk about?* A transformative mediator might also check in with the parties before summarizing, by saying something along the lines of, *I think it might be helpful for me to summarize what I'm hearing from the two of you. Would that be okay?*

A mediator might also check in by highlighting parties' decisions about their level of participation in the conversation. For instance, if a party has been quiet throughout the process, the mediator might say, *John, I noticed that you've been pretty quiet the last few minutes. No pressure, but I just wanted to remind you that you're welcome to speak up, as far as I'm concerned.*

So a check-in reminds the parties that they're at a potential decision point, and that these are their decisions to make. Unlike facilitative or evaluative mediators, questions transformative mediators ask are not designed to gather information from the parties. For instance, they would not ask for a list of the parties' assets or what time their child gets home from school. Instead, transformative mediators use questions solely to check in and remind parties that they have choice about what's happening.[14]

The mediator uses all three practices (*reflection*, *summary*, and the *check-in*) to support the parties. This support is designed to put the parties in the best position to do what the transformative theory assumes people generally *want* to do, which is to make empowerment and recognition shifts – to move from the vicious circle, where they are feeling weak and self-absorbed, to the virtuous circle, where they are feeling stronger and more responsive to each other. The mediator assumes that, as the parties move in the direction of the virtuous circle, they will be increasingly able to make clear decisions. This will likely increase their willingness and ability to work together and find solutions to their problems, without being nudged or directed to do so by the mediator.

Transformative mediators usually meet with the parties together (i.e., a joint session), but they also welcome the parties to request individual meetings with the mediator. A party may want to bounce an idea off the mediator, think through their options, or simply share views that they're reluctant to share in front of the other party. The mediator primarily reflects the party and helps them decide their next steps. The mediator's goal in an individual session is the same as during a joint session – to support the parties as they express themselves and make their own choices.

Unlike many evaluative and some facilitative mediators, the transformative mediator generally does not pass messages between parties; nor do they use information gleaned during an individual session to try to lead the parties in any direction – toward an agreement or away from an agreement, or even toward empathy and understanding. Because the role of the transformative mediator is to support the parties as they make their own decisions, the mediator is comfortable keeping information shared by a party in an individual session confidential. Transformative mediators do not view it as their role to make decisions for the parties about what to share or when to share it.

The transformative mediator's commitment to solely support the parties, and to refrain from judging their decisions, extends to situations where the mediator has decided to withdraw from a case. Rather than pointing to the parties' actions as a reason to withdraw, the transformative mediator solely attends to their own ability to support both parties. The mediator might notice that they feel strongly aligned with, or protective toward, one of the parties, and that they (the mediator) are not behaving in a way that is fully supportive of both parties.

The mediator's inability to support both parties could be due to something truly destructive happening between the parties, or it could be because the parties' dynamic is triggering a traumatic memory from the mediator's own life. Regardless of the cause (which the mediator cannot know with certainty), if the mediator believes that continuing to mediate would likely do more harm than good, they will simply say to the parties, *I'm sorry, but I don't think I can help you any longer.*[15]

THEORY AND GOALS, REVISITED

The aim of the transformative mediator is not to get the parties to an agreement; nor is it to get them to *do* anything. Instead, a high-quality outcome is one in which each party experiences an increased sense of empowerment. While the transformative mediator also values recognition shifts (movement in the direction of the parties seeing each other more clearly), the mediator does not try to move the parties toward recognition directly. Instead, the transformative mediator sees recognition as the natural result of empowerment, which is itself the natural result of being supported throughout the process.

While many mediators view it as the mediator's job to control the process, including "who talks to whom about what and how,"[16] that's not how transformative mediators view their role. From the perspective of the transformative mediator, the mediator's role is to follow the parties throughout the process, and support them as they make their own decisions, every step of the way.

This is not to say that settlements or improved relationships are not relevant to the transformative mediator. In fact, the belief that transformative practices often lead to these valued outcomes may be one reason that many transformative mediators embrace this approach. However, the transformative mediator believes that the parties are in a better position than the mediator to know what's right for them, including the terms of their agreement, if any, and the terms of their relationship going forward, if any.[17] Therefore, the transformative mediator does not focus on these outcomes.

Because transformative mediators do not assume they know what good decisions look like in any particular situation, they are not tempted to adjust the process as they go in order to get the parties to any particular place. In fact, the transformative mediator would not even nudge the parties toward the virtuous circle, for instance, by asking them to look at things from each other's perspective.[18] According to transformative theory, any attempt to push the parties into viewing the situation from the other's perspective would be futile, as any lasting realizations would need to come from the parties themselves, and from a place of empowerment.[19]

In the same vein, the transformative mediator refrains from attempting to correct any perceived power imbalances,[20] or from trying to move the parties away from an "unfair" agreement, viewing these attempts as more likely to backfire than to offer any actual protection.[21] Instead, the transformative mediator solely supports the parties, assuming that if they are going to get to a stronger, more responsive place, this is the process most likely to help them get there.

Similarly, transformative mediators believe that if a sustainable, workable agreement is available to the parties, this is the process most likely to help them reach it. Transformative theory assumes that any commitment resulting from a party being pushed or pressured will inevitably be a weak commitment, whereas one that is freely reached will be much stronger, and therefore more likely to "stick."[22] And if such an agreement is not available, this process will allow the parties to see that more clearly and make whatever decisions they need to make next.

So that's transformative mediation in a nutshell. Our next stop on this tour is an approach that shares features in common with each of the three approaches we've discussed so far (evaluative, facilitative, and transformative), and this is the understanding-based model of mediation.

1   Bush, R. A. B., & Folger, J. P. (2005). *The promise of mediation: The transformative approach to conflict.* San Francisco, CA: Jossey-Bass.

2   See Della Noce, D., Antes, J. R., & Saul, J. A., 2004. Identifying practice competence in transformative mediators: An interactive rating scale assessment model. *Ohio State Journal on Dispute Resolution, 19*(3), 1005-1058 (describing a process whereby one can take a test and get certified as a transformative mediator). The certification process ensures that those who are certified would agree about the goals and practices, although others in the field may be confused about the model. See Bush, R. A. B., & Folger, J. P. (2013). Response to Condlin's critique of transformative mediation. *Cardozo Journal of Conflict Resolution, 15*(1), 231-241 (explaining that Condlin misrepresented the transformative model).

3   See Bush & Folger (2005); see also Bush, R. A. B. & Pope, S. G. (2002). Changing the quality of conflict interaction: The principles and practice of transformative mediation. *Pepperdine Dispute Resolution Law Journal, 3*(1), 67-96.

4   Bush & Folger (2005), at p. 56; Bush & Pope (2002), at p. 82.

5   Bush & Folger (2005), at p. 60.

6   Bush & Folger (2005), at p. 55.

7   Bush & Pope (2002), at pp. 88-89.

8   Bush & Pope (2002), at p. 89.

9   Bush & Pope (2002), at p. 89.

10 Bush & Folger (2005), at p. 144.

11 See Bush, R. A. B. (2010). Taking self-determination seriously: The centrality of empowerment in transformative mediation. In J. P. Folger, R. A. B. Bush, & D. J. Della Noce (Eds.), *Transformative Mediation: A Sourcebook* (pp. 51-72). (n.p.): Institute for the Study of Conflict Transformation, Inc., at p. 66.

12 Bush & Pope (2002), at p. 89.

13 Bush & Pope (2002), at p. 90.

14 Bush & Pope (2002), at p. 90.

15 Simon, D., West, T. (2019, July 24). Transformative mediation - Theory and practice [On-Demand CLE]. *American Bar Association, Section on Dispute Resolution,* at 50:45-51:50. Retrieved from https://www.americanbar.org/events-cle/ecd/ondemand/377910204/

16 I'm borrowing the phrase used to describe transformative dialogue, coined by Erik Cleven. Cleven, E. (2011). Who needs to talk to whom about what and how? Transformative dialogue in settings of ethnopolitical conflict. *Institute for the Study of Conflict Transformation White Papers.*

17 Bush & Pope (2002), at p. 93.

18 See Bush (2010), noting that early efforts to practice and articulate the transformative approach actually did entail some direction from the mediator, who nudged the parties toward recognition of each other's perspectives. The model has since evolved, however, and is now purely supportive of the parties' own efforts to move in the direction from the vicious circle to the virtuous circle.

19 See Bush (2010), at p. 66.

20 Some mediators might attempt to "power balance" by asking a party to speak up who has been quiet. In contrast, a transformative mediator would reflect the party's silence, and then offer an opportunity to speak, as discussed in the earlier section describing the *check-in*. The mediator would make it clear that the party could choose to speak up (or not), and that the mediator would support whatever choice the party made. So while the transformative mediator values the goal of increased *empowerment* for all parties, a shift in that direction can be evident in a party's clear decision to remain quiet, as much as in a clear decision to speak up.

21 See Bush, R. A. B., & Folger, J. P. (2012). Mediation and social justice: Risks and opportunities. *Ohio State Journal on Dispute Resolution, 27*(1), 1-51.

22 See Bush (2010), at p. 66.

5. UNDERSTANDING-BASED MEDIATION

Understanding-based mediation, like the transformative approach, would be considered a mediation model. There is consistency in what people mean when they use this label, and a theoretical basis for the practices these mediators use. Gary Friedman and Jack Himmelstein lay all of this out in the model's foundational text, *Challenging Conflict: Mediation Through Understanding*.[1]

THEORY AND GOALS

In *Challenging Conflict*, Friedman and Himmelstein explain the theory behind this approach, which is that misunderstanding – often misunderstanding the motives, desires, and perspectives of the other party – plays a significant role in keeping people embroiled in the conflict trap.[2] Therefore, understanding is the key to resolving conflicts. This includes understanding one's own perspective, along with the perspective of the other. This also includes understanding the practical realities of the situation, such as everyone's income and expenses, along with the legal realities, or how courts handle similar situations.[3]

Like the evaluative mediator (particularly of the *Judge* variety), the understanding-based mediator views legal precedent as relevant. These mediators believe that to be truly informed, the parties must be aware of the legal landscape, and the understanding-based mediator is comfortable sharing those legal realities with the parties.[4] However, the mediator also encourages the parties to use any other criteria they view as relevant when making decisions, such as their own sense of fairness or prior agreements they made with each other.[5]

The understanding-based mediator values the goal of reaching a high-quality outcome and believes it's their role to guide the parties toward an informed agreement that meets everyone's important needs. But the agreement is not the understanding-based mediator's only priority, and certainly not at any cost. As the Friedman and Himmelstein explain, "For us, success is not achieved when agreements are not solid or were not the product of joint decision making."[6] Instead, the understanding-based mediator would value a mediation "where some authentic exchange occurred that represented an important movement between the parties,"[7] whether an agreement was reached or not. Understanding-based mediators, like transformative mediators, recognize that *how* an agreement is reached may be more important to the parties than *if* an agreement is reached.[8]

Like the facilitative mediator, the understanding-based mediator uses interest-based problem-solving strategies, meaning they attempt to help the parties understand their own, and the other party's, important needs and wants.[9] However, the understanding-based mediator takes this line of inquiry deeper by exploring the meaning and emotional significance of each party's interests.

Returning to an example from our discussion of facilitative mediation, a divorcing wife may want a relatively high proportion of liquid assets (her position) because of her *interest* in taking additional career-related training, with the eventual goal of being able to support herself without help from her spouse. The understanding-based mediator might explore this interest further and discover the wife's underlying value of *independence*.

This exploration is designed to help each party understand their own, and each other's, needs on a deeper level, which should then increase the parties' willingness and ability to find solutions that work well for everyone.

Like the transformative mediator, the understanding-based mediator views conflict as self-perpetuating and cyclical in nature, and views clarity – seeing both oneself and the other party more clearly – as playing an important role in escaping the "conflict trap."[10]

Understanding-based mediators therefore do not shy away from potential disagreements; nor do they try to steer the conversation away from the past or from strong emotions.[11]

Also like the transformative mediator, the understanding-based mediator views humans as social animals who value their own autonomy in addition to their connections with each other. Mediators of both approaches see the impulse to work through conflict as "a natural part of the human condition."[12] That is, none of us feel good when trapped in conflict, and we all yearn to find a way out of it.

Unlike the transformative mediator, the understanding-based mediator tries to move the parties out of the conflict trap directly. For instance, the understanding-based mediator may ask the parties to think about and share their reasons for wanting to work through the conflict together.[13]

The understanding-based mediator might also try to move the conversation in a direction that the mediator thinks is more likely to be productive than the current conversation. For example, the mediator might say, "I understand how angry you are with him. But instead of characterizing Henry, I prefer you talk about your own experience. It will be easier for me to understand you, and less inflammatory."[14]

The understanding-based mediator's comfort with direction may stem from their tendency to view the mediator as a party to the process.[15] This is in sharp contrast to the transformative mediator's view of their role, which is to solely support the parties' conversation.

An example of this difference can be seen in how mediators practicing the two approaches would respond if an aspect of the parties' plan had not yet been ironed out. A transformative mediator would make note of the missing piece and mention it as one possible topic of conversation. The transformative mediator would make it clear that it was the parties' decision if they wanted to clarify that aspect of their plan, saying, "I don't have to be clear about that, but you might want to [be]."[16]

In contrast, the understanding-based mediator would ask the parties clarifying questions to ensure that the plan was clear to everyone. The understanding-based mediator views the *mediator's* understanding of the parties, in addition to the parties' understanding of each other, as central to the process.

HOW DO THEY DO IT?

Sharing goals with the other three approaches we've discussed so far, the understanding-based model also shares some of their practices. As you might imagine, practices aimed at increasing the participants' understanding (of themselves, each other, and the situation) play a feature role in this model.

Looping

A key practice in the understanding-based process is reflection, and their method of reflecting is a four-step process they've termed, "looping."[17] The goals of looping are to increase the mediator's understanding of each party, allow each party to be heard, and help the parties hear each other. When looping the parties, the mediator follows four steps in this order: "1. Understand each party; 2. Express that understanding; 3. Seek confirmation from the parties that they feel understood by the mediator; 4. Receive that confirmation."[18] Let's break these steps down.

Understand each party

The first step of looping is to listen to the speaker with the goal of understanding what they are saying. This sounds simple, but given how rarely we listen to someone without thinking about whether we agree or what they should do, this type of listening actually takes some effort. So in this step, the mediator attempts to suspend those judgements and to instead focus solely on understanding what the speaker is trying to express.

Express that understanding

Step two is where reflection comes in. In this step, the mediator reflects what the speaker expressed, using the mediator's own words. The mediator uses their own words when reflecting because words can be interpreted in different ways, and the mediator wants to ensure – and demonstrate – that the mediator really did understand what the speaker was trying to say.

Seek confirmation from the parties that they feel understood by the mediator

In the third step, the mediator asks the reflected party if the mediator's reflection was accurate. The mediator might do this any number of ways, such as by asking, *Did I understand you correctly?* Or *Did I get that right?* Or just, *Right?* The mediator's goal is to make it clear to the reflected party that the mediator is interested in knowing whether or not their reflection hit the mark.

Receive that confirmation

In the fourth step, the reflected party responds. So before moving on, the mediator waits for the party to confirm that the mediator did, in fact, get it right.

This step also provides an opportunity to return to the first step (understand each party) since the reflected party will likely add information at this point. If the mediator misunderstood what was said, the party might say, *Actually, what I meant was…* and then correct the mediator. Or the party might say, *Yeah, that's basically it, but…* and offer a clarification. Or, if the mediator's reflection really hit the mark, the party might say, *Yeah, exactly, AND…* and then add more.

If the party does any of these things (corrects, clarifies, or simply shares more), the mediator goes back to the first step and listens to this – whatever the party is now saying – with the goal of understanding. So the mediator keeps *looping* through these steps until the party has shared as much as they would like to share at that point.

So looping is another way to accomplish the goals of reflection, which we discussed in the section on transformative mediation – it gives parties an opportunity to be heard, to clarify their thoughts, and to hear each other more clearly.[19] Additionally, looping demonstrates that the *mediator* understood what the party was saying, which is part of the understanding-based process.

The mediator uses this practice of looping throughout the mediation process, which tends to proceed through the following five stages: 1) Contracting; 2) Defining the problem; 3) Working through the conflict; 4) Developing and evaluating options; and 5) Reaching agreement.[20]

Contracting

During the contracting stage, the mediator, parties, and counsel figure out if and how they will work together.[21] The understanding-based mediator wants to make sure that everyone involved is on the same page from the beginning, and that the parties (and their counsel) are making an informed decision to work with the mediator.[22]

The mediator would make it clear to the parties and counsel that, in the understanding-based process, the parties remain in the same room with each other, rather than communicating from separate rooms via the mediator or their attorneys. The mediator would explain that, in their view, each party's understanding of the other's needs and perspective is essential, so the parties need to be able to hear directly from each other.

The mediator also explains that the parties are expected to make joint decisions and to share all relevant information with each other. In the understanding-based process, relevant information includes information about the law, in addition to information about the parties' needs and interests. The mediator explains that their goal is to ensure that all of the parties' decisions are informed, and that the decisions meet everyone's important needs as well as possible.

Defining the problem

Once the participants and mediator have decided to work together, the mediator's first goal is to define and frame the problem. In this stage, the mediator tries to understand the parties' different perspectives on the relevant issues so the mediator can frame the problem in a way that takes all perspectives into account.[23]

In a dispute between business partners, for example, the mediator may discover that one party is concerned about the financial stability of the business, while the other is concerned about maintaining a work-life balance. The mediator might frame such a problem like this: *The question is how to ensure that the business is profitable while maintaining a comfortable workplace culture.*

Working through the conflict

Once the problem has been defined, and the areas of disagreement have become clear, the understanding-based mediator tries to draw out the parties' motivations for working through the conflict together. The mediator wants to ensure that the parties are willing and able to sit with the tension of disagreement, so that the process will run off the parties' "steam," rather than the mediator's.[24]

The mediator recognizes that, not only do parties care about their own individual goals, they also often care about the relationship with the other party, and any joint projects they have. For example, the parties may be co-parents who will continue to raise a child together post-divorce, or members of a symphony who value the music that they make together. So when tapping the parties' motivations for working through the conflict, the mediator aims to support each party's autonomy, while also honoring the parties' connections with each other.[25]

Developing and evaluating options

As mentioned earlier, understanding-based mediators are also interest-based mediators. They try to help the parties get clearer on their important needs, or why they want what they want, and then use the parties' different interests to create value that can benefit all parties.[26]

Uncovering interests

As a first step in developing options, the understanding-based mediator tries to find out the needs and motivations behind the parties' positions.[27] With this goal in mind, the mediator asks each party *why* they want what they want. If the party seems to be having trouble identifying her needs or interests, the mediator may make some suggestions. The mediator might say, "I imagine if I were you that it might be important to me that..."[28] and suggest a possible need or two.

The mediator then *loops* the parties' responses to help them frame each of their interests in a way that is likely to generate effective, workable solutions. Each interest would need to be broad enough to allow for several possible solutions, but not so broad that the options are virtually unlimited.

For example, when discussing a party's preferred living situation, naming the interest as *the family home* would be too narrow, whereas *a house* would be too broad. Instead, relevant interests would likely include specificity in terms of the approximate square footage and/or number of rooms, along with some location-related preferences (e.g., under a 20-minute commute to work/school, within walking distance of grocery stores).

According to the understanding-based approach, each interest would need to be framed in a positive, future-oriented way – a frame that points to a benefit to at least one party, rather than a cost to the other. Continuing with the example discussed in the facilitative and transformative sections, if the husband said he wanted his wife to stop putting him down in front of the kids, the understanding-based mediator might frame this interest as a need for *respectful communication in front of the kids* rather than *wife stops putting husband down in front of the kids*.

Friedman and Himmelstein refer to the framing of interests as "a negotiation between the mediator and the party whose interests are being articulated."[29] They assert that no interest should be listed until both the mediator and the party with the interest agree to the framing.

Brainstorming options

After uncovering each party's interests and listing them on a flip chart, the next step for the understanding-based mediator would be to help the parties brainstorm ideas that "create value" or "expand the pie."[30] In this step, the mediator encourages the parties to think of options that will make at least one party better off without making the other party worse off. For example, a mediator might encourage divorcing parents to collaborate in a way that would minimize their total tax obligation. This would "expand the pie" by putting more money in the hands of the family, which could then be shared between the parents and with their children.

When brainstorming, the mediator ensures that all of the options are listed in one place, without names attached. This is meant to help the parties identify possible solutions without feeling like they're committing to any option they happen to mention. The mediator might offer additional options, as well. They would be sure to offer more than one option in order to prevent the parties from attaching extra weight to the mediator's ideas.

Evaluating options

After identifying a number of options in the brainstorming stage, the mediator asks each party to indicate how acceptable they find each option.[31] For example, the parties might be asked to put each option in one of the following three categories: very acceptable, possibly acceptable, or unacceptable.

After ruling out options unacceptable to either party, the parties then would evaluate the remaining options by asking themselves how well each option met their identified interests or needs. The goal here is to home in on the options that best satisfied each party's important needs.

Reaching agreement

In the final stage of the process, the mediator helps the parties negotiate an agreement.[32] This generally involves having the parties make offers and explain why their offer works well for everyone involved. If the parties' offers are far apart, the mediator might suggest the parties next make simultaneous offers, in writing, and share them with the mediator before sharing them with each other.

The mediator will then review each offer to determine if it is reasonable enough to share with the other party. The mediator is trying to avoid putting either party in a vulnerable position, where they might be worried about making a move in the other's party's direction without having the move reciprocated.

During this final stage, the mediator tries to ensure that no one falls into any of the common traps that can occur when the end is in sight, and the parties are tempted to rush the process. The understanding-based mediator also tries to guard against the mediator's own temptation to solve the parties' problem, in addition to any tendency the parties' lawyers might have to take over the negotiations and speak for the parties. The understanding-based mediator wants to ensure that each party is speaking up for their own interests while also keeping the other party's interests in mind.

The mediator's goal in this final stage is to help the parties negotiate an agreement that is acceptable to all parties (and acceptable *enough* to the mediator). To the understanding-based mediator, an agreement is acceptable if it 1) meets the parties' important interests, and 2) is workable, given the legal and financial realities along with other relevant aspects of the situation.

THEORY AND GOALS, REVISITED

Unlike the transformative mediator, who follows and supports the parties as they make their own decisions about both the process and the outcome, the understanding-based mediator views the mediator as a party to the process, with their own understanding and perspective being relevant. A principle of this model is that the mediator and the parties all "proceed by agreement,"[33] meaning every step of the process must be acceptable to all parties and to the mediator.

At times, of course, the mediator's sense of what the parties should do or consider will conflict with the parties' sense of what they should do or consider. For example, as the parties are homing in on a solution, the mediator may believe they're ignoring practical realities that will make the solution unworkable. In such a case, the mediator will urge the parties to consider those realities, and will "press the point"[34] if the parties are still not considering the realities enough to satisfy the mediator.

Ultimately, the mediator will not go forward unless and until the parties proceed in a way that makes the mediator comfortable. So while the understanding-based mediator would not pressure the parties *into* an agreement, as the evaluative *Dealmaker* might, the understanding-based mediator may pressure the parties *away* from an agreement, as the evaluative *Judge* might.[35]

So that's the understanding-based approach in a nutshell. In the next chapter, we'll cover narrative mediation, the fifth and final mediation approach to be discussed in this guide.

1   Friedman, G. & Himmelstein, J. (2008). *Challenging conflict: Mediation through understanding.* Chicago, IL: American Bar Association.

2   Friedman & Himmelstein (2008), at pp. 10-11.

3   Friedman & Himmelstein (2008), at pp. pp. 139, 163-164.

4   Friedman, G. J. (1993). *A guide to divorce mediation: How to reach a fair, legal settlement at a fraction of the cost.* New York, NY: Workman Publishing, at p. 35.

5   Friedman (1993), at pp. 48-53.

6   Friedman & Himmelstein (2008), at p. 271.

7   Friedman & Himmelstein (2008), at p. 271.

8   Friedman & Himmelstein (2008), at p. 272.

9   Friedman & Himmelstein (2008), at pp. 127-133.

10 Friedman & Himmelstein (2008), at p. 69.

11 Friedman & Himmelstein (2008), at p. 66.

12 Friedman & Himmelstein (2008), at p. 82.

13 Friedman & Himmelstein (2008), at pp. 83-84.

14 Friedman & Himmelstein (2008), at p. 212.

15 Menkel-Meadow, C. (2011). Comments on case 12.2. In E. Waldman (Ed.), *Mediation ethics: Cases and commentaries* (pp. 320-327). San Francisco, CA: Jossey-Bass, at p. 326.

16 Catalyst IpF - Initiating Positive Futures. (2017, July 6). *Purple house conversations 2 of 2* [Video file], at 14:17. Retrieved from https://www.youtube.com/watch?v=l5IZTIixtQk

17 Friedman & Himmelstein (2008), at p. 68.

18 Friedman & Himmelstein (2008), at p. 68.

19 Friedman & Himmelstein (2008), at p. 69.

20 Friedman & Himmelstein (2008), at p. 39.

21 Friedman & Himmelstein (2008), at pp. 52-57.

22 Friedman & Himmelstein (2008), at p. 52.

23 Friedman & Himmelstein (2008), at pp. 63-64.

24 Friedman & Himmelstein (2008), at p. 84.

25 Friedman & Himmelstein (2008), at pp. 92-94.

26 Friedman & Himmelstein (2008), at pp. 127-33.

27 Friedman & Himmelstein (2008), at pp. 129-31

28 Friedman & Himmelstein (2008), at p. 128.

29 Friedman & Himmelstein (2008), at p. 129.

30 Friedman & Himmelstein (2008), at pp. 242-43.

31 Friedman & Himmelstein (2008), at pp. 268-70.

32 Friedman & Himmelstein (2008), at pp. 272-73.

33 Friedman & Himmelstein (2008), at p. 42.

34 Friedman & Himmelstein (2008), at p. 266.

35 Friedman (1993), at p. 30.

6. NARRATIVE MEDIATION

Narrative mediation, like the transformative and understanding-based approaches, is a mediation model, with a theoretical basis and foundational text. John Winslade and Gerald Monk describe the theory and practices of the narrative approach in *Narrative Mediation: A New Approach to Conflict Resolution.*[1]

THEORY AND GOALS

As you might imagine from the name, the narrative approach emphasizes stories. Narrative mediators assume that the stories we've been told and that we tell ourselves shape our identities and form our relationships.[2] In doing so, these stories directly and indirectly affect our experience of conflict.

Our stories can include "background stories," which are the broad, general stories about individuals, groups, and society that we picked up from our family or from the larger culture.[3] Our stories can also be specific, such as stories we tell ourselves about the needs, motivations, and capacities of ourselves and others in a given situation.

In a conflict situation, we might tell ourselves that the other person was being unfair and selfish, and that they can't be trusted – stories that magnify the conflict and keep it going. Alternatively, we might tell ourselves that there was a misunderstanding, and that the other person didn't mean to do us harm – stories that minimize or reduce the conflict. Narrative mediators try to uncover and challenge the conflict-perpetuating stories, and then help the parties to create peace-promoting stories.

While the narrative mediator hopes to help the parties resolve their conflict, the mediator's main goal is to facilitate respectful relations between the parties, and toward third parties. Third parties can include coworkers, neighbors, a divorcing couple's children, and even members of society at large.

The goals of the narrative mediator extend beyond the conflict itself, and beyond the parties directly affected by the conflict. Specifically, the narrative mediator values the goal of furthering social justice. According to Winslade and Monk, "The mediator can either promote social justice and attend to equity and fairness, or reinforce unjust dominant cultural practices."[4] The founders acknowledge that the narrative approach is not a neutral one.[5]

The narrative mediator's social justice goals are embedded in their process and outcome goals. For narrative mediators, a high-quality process addresses potential power imbalances (e.g., between parents and children, or between social groups based on race or gender) and is inclusive of affected third parties. For example, narrative mediators will encourage divorcing parents to consider the wishes and desires of the children and may suggest that the children attend at least one session.[6]

Likewise, a narrative mediator's version of a high-quality outcome includes reducing group-based power differentials, not just for the sake of the parties or directly affected third parties, but also for the sake of society. For example, if a party came in with a story suggesting that a woman's place was in the home, the mediator would try to lead the party toward a story that opened more options for women, assuming that this would affect the party's treatment of all women.

The narrative approach encourages the mediator to promote their version of a healthy relationship, perhaps because the narrative approach to mediation stems from the narrative approach to psychotherapy (referred to as "narrative therapy").[7] In New Zealand, where the narrative approach was founded, mediations that occur in the context of the family court system are often conducted by counselors and are referred to as "counseling." It seems that, at least in the family context, the boundary between narrative mediation and therapy is blurred.[8]

HOW DO THEY DO IT?

A narrative mediation moves through roughly three phases. It begins with the "engagement" phase, in which the mediator aims to build a relationship with each party. This sets the stage for the "deconstructing the conflict-saturated story" phase, in which the mediator helps the parties deconstruct, or break down, their conflict stories. Next, in the "constructing the alternative story" phase, the mediator tries to help the parties create stories of cooperation and peace in place of the conflict-saturated stories.

The engagement phase

The mediator's goal in the engagement phase is to connect with the parties and set the stage for constructive, respectful conversations throughout the mediation. Conversations during this phase often occur in separate meetings (where the mediator meets with one party at a time). These meetings give the mediator a chance to establish a relationship with each party, along with an opportunity for each party to tell their own version of the story to the mediator.[9] Given how significant storytelling is to the narrative approach, this is an essential part of the process.

In the engagement phase, the mediator asks each party to tell their own story of the conflict, along with any relevant "background stories."[10] The mediator does not try to find out what *really* happened in the conflict since narrative mediators believe conflict is perpetuated (or resolved) through the parties' stories themselves.[11] Instead, the mediator reflects and summarizes what the party shared to show the party that the mediator is interested in, and respectful of, their perspective.[12]

Deconstructing the conflict-saturated story

Once the mediator has established rapport, their main goals are to "separate the parties from the conflict-saturated story,"[13] and to make room for new stories. In the process, the mediator tries to *externalize* the conflict, which is captured by the catchphrase, "The person is not the problem; the problem is the problem."[14] Throughout the mediation, the mediator refers to the conflict as if it were an independent entity with a will of its own, for example by asking, "So, how did this argument catch you both in its clutches?"[15] The mediator may even ask the parties what they would name the conflict. [16]

Also in this phase, the mediator tries to motivate the parties to rid themselves of the conflict by drawing their attention to the negative effects the conflict has had on them, and on others. The mediator asks the parties to think about how the conflict has affected various aspects of their lives, such as their relationships, career, finances, attitudes, and ability to relax. The mediator also asks the parties to think about how long the conflict has been going on, and how serious the effects have been. The mediator may ask the parties to rate the seriousness of the problem, and to tell a story illustrating the effects of the conflict.[17]

The mediator also challenges the conflict stories by asking the parties questions to help them see how their stories may be incomplete. For example, the mediator might ask, "As you speak about trust, I wonder what has influenced your thinking on this issue?"[18] The mediator might also suggest themes for the parties to consider, for instance by asking, "Is there a gendered aspect to this idea of trust? Would it take on a different shape if you were a different gender?"[19] The mediator's goal is to get the parties questioning the assumptions that underlie the conflict-saturated stories, thereby reducing the stories' influence.

In addition to focusing on the parties' stories that are specific to the conflict, the mediator challenges the broader background stories the parties may be carrying into the conflict. Because the narrative mediator views their role as promoting social justice, the mediator pays special attention to stories they see as perpetuating group-based power differences, such as those based on race, gender, or age.[20]

The narrative mediator is especially attuned to stories that reflect the "dominant discourse,"[21] including assumptions parties have about their own and others' rights and responsibilities. For example, in a conflict between a former employee (Mark), who started his own business, and the entrepreneur (Penny), who previously employed Mark, the mediator may ask Penny, "[B]ecause you feel you discovered Mark, how much do you think he needs to repay you in loyalty before he develops his creativity in other ways?" The mediator may ask Mark, "[W]hat silenced you from discussing with Penny your intention to take some entrepreneurial steps of your own?"[22]

Recognizing that certain probing questions may make the parties uncomfortable, the narrative mediator will generally ask these questions in individual sessions. The mediator assumes that each party will feel less vulnerable responding to these questions without the other party in the room.[23]

The mediator also challenges early family stories, for example, about the role of a father in the lives of his children. With the goal of increasing a father's involvement with his children following a divorce, the mediator may ask questions such as, "As you look back on your history with your own father, how would you describe your relationship with him?" or "Where did your father learn about fathering?"[24] The mediator may follow these questions with: "Are you compelled to repeat your own early history of having your father absent from your life or do you want to begin to take a stand against history repeating itself?"[25]

If you're thinking, *Now, some of those questions sound like leading questions*, you're not wrong. As mentioned earlier, the narrative mediator does not value neutrality, and instead views their role as promoting certain relationships and challenging others, particularly when the relationships include group-based power differentials.

Constructing the alternative story

In the third phase, the narrative mediator tries to help the parties replace the conflict stories with alternative stories – stories "of respect, cooperation, understanding, and peace."[26] The mediator primarily asks questions to direct the parties' attention to evidence supporting these alternative stories. And as the parties make decisions consistent with these stories, the mediator documents their progress.

Asking questions

The narrative mediator begins the third phase of the process by asking the parties about times things were going well between them, despite the conflict.

For example, the mediator might ask, "Do any recent occasions stand out for you in which hurt feelings and blame did not completely destroy your efforts at searching for a solution?"[27] The mediator may then encourage the parties to think about their role in creating these experiences. For instance, the mediator might ask, "How do you explain that you were able to be more in charge of blame, humiliation, hurt feelings, or injustice than you initially thought?"[28]

The narrative mediator also uses questions to motivate and inspire the parties to improve themselves and their relationship with each other. The mediator might ask, "What does this tell you about yourself that you otherwise would not have known?" or, "If most of the time you were able to talk civilly and respectfully about things, as you have been doing today, what would your relationship be like?"[29]

Next, the narrative mediator will ask the parties to think about future steps they could take, and how others would likely react to those steps. The mediator might ask the parties to imagine what other people (e.g., their children, employees, customers, neighbors) would say if they were asked to weigh in (e.g., "If your children were witness to these discussions, who would be most excited about this change in direction?"[30]). The mediator is trying to ground the parties' decisions in their social context, assuming this will strengthen the parties' commitment to their decisions.

Documenting progress
Unlike approaches that primarily aim for an agreement, the narrative approach sees the agreement as the natural outgrowth of all the phases that preceded it. According to this theory, once the relational issues have been addressed, the parties should be in a good position to have a productive conversation about how

to resolve the dispute. Therefore, the mediator uses documentation to solidify and reinforce the parties' progress, viewing, "written agreements [as] tools for ongoing narrative development rather than goals of the process."[31]

To document the parties' progress, the mediator writes letters to the parties outlining any large or small decisions the parties made, along with some context for the decisions. For example, the mediator might write, "Danny, you identified that Lance needed a junior assistant to take some routine pressures off him."[32] They may follow this with "Lance, you appreciated this as a helpful suggestion from Danny that would make a difference to your feelings of being appreciated and your ability to make decisions on your own."[33]

The mediator would then pose questions for the parties to consider and discuss at the next session, such as, "Do these developments and agreements mean that you are starting to reformulate your working relationship in ways that you would prefer?"[34]

THEORY AND GOALS, REVISITED

According to the narrative theory, the three phases of the process (engagement, deconstructing the conflict-saturated story, and constructing the alternative story) set the stage for solution-focused conversations, which may lead to an agreement if the parties choose to go in that direction. So the narrative mediator does not directly steer the parties toward an agreement, nor even toward specific problem-solving steps, but instead tries to foster a cooperative spirit among the parties.

The narrative mediator assumes this spirit of cooperation will lead to constructive conversations that are more likely to result in an agreement, an assumption shared with the transformative approach. Unlike the transformative approach, however, the narrative mediator directs the parties' conversation, primarily through the use of questions.

The narrative approach shares with the *Judge* version of the evaluative approach a tendency to use evaluations to ensure that the parties' decisions are acceptable to the mediator. But instead of using the law or the parties' stated interests as yardsticks, the narrative mediator uses the mediator's sense of what constitutes respectful, healthy relations between people when assessing both the process and outcome of the mediation.

So that's the narrative approach in a nutshell. What's next?

1   Winslade, J. & Monk, G. (2001). *Narrative Mediation: A new approach to conflict resolution.* San Francisco, CA: Jossey-Bass.

2   Winslade & Monk (2001), at pp. xii-xiii (the narrative approach to both mediation and therapy has its roots in postmodernism and social constructivism, philosophies that are beyond the scope of this text).

3   Winslade & Monk (2001), at p. 53.

4   Winslade & Monk (2001), at p. 100.

5   Winslade & Monk (2001), at p. 101.

6   Winslade & Monk (2001), at p. 21.

7   Winslade & Monk (2001), at p. 253.

8   Winslade & Monk (2001), at p. 225.

9   Winslade & Monk (2001), at pp. 139-40.

10 Winslade & Monk (2001), at p. 53.

11 Winslade & Monk (2001), at pp. 70-71.

12 Winslade & Monk (2001), at p. 64.

13 Winslade & Monk (2001), at p. 72.

14 Winslade & Monk (2001), at p. 143.

15 Winslade & Monk (2001), at p. 144.

16 Winslade & Monk (2001), at p. 147.

17 Winslade & Monk (2001), at pp. 152-53.

18 Winslade & Monk (2001), at p. 142.

19 Winslade & Monk (2001), at p. 142.

20 Winslade & Monk (2001), at pp. 96-98.

21 Winslade & Monk (2001), at p. 80.

22 Winslade & Monk (2001), at p. 81.

23 Winslade & Monk (2001), at p. 80.

24 Winslade & Monk (2001), at p. 224.

25 Winslade & Monk (2001), at pp. 224-25.

26 Winslade & Monk (2001), at p. 250.

27 Winslade & Monk (2001), at p. 87.

28 Winslade & Monk (2001), at pp. 87-88.

29 Winslade & Monk (2001), at p. 88.

30 Winslade & Monk (2001), at p. 89.

31 Winslade & Monk (2001), at p. 228.

32 Winslade & Monk (2001), at p. 229.

33 Winslade & Monk (2001), at p. 230.

34 Winslade & Monk (2001), at p. 230.

7. NEXT STEPS

Congratulations! You made it through an overview of five (and a half) approaches to mediation. As you've seen, there is quite a bit of overlap among, and variation within, the approaches, along with some stark differences between them. Many of the differences stem from the different goals mediators value and prioritize.

A BRIEF RECAP

As we discussed, mediators' goals largely fall within the following four categories: 1) Reach an agreement (any agreement); 2) reach a high-quality agreement; 3) reach a high-quality outcome (other than an agreement); and 4) participate in a high-quality process. Now let's review the goals of the different approaches, and how these goals shape the mediators' practices.

Evaluative Mediation

We discussed two different versions of evaluative mediation: *Dealmakers* and *Judges*. While both are willing to share their evaluations with the parties, they do so with different goals in mind. The *Dealmakers* prioritize the goal of helping the parties reach an agreement – any agreement – by (almost) any means necessary. They therefore strategically share their evaluations of each party's arguments to move each party toward the other's position and toward an agreement.

The *Judges*, on the other hand, prioritize the goal of helping the parties reach a *high-quality* agreement (in the mediator's eyes). These mediators share their evaluations of the parties' joint decisions in order to move them *away* from an agreement that does not meet the mediator's sense of fairness or justice, and *toward* an agreement that the mediator thinks is appropriate.

Facilitative Mediation

Facilitative mediators, like the *Dealmakers*, tend to prioritize the goal of helping the parties reach an agreement, without evaluating the agreement itself. However, instead of using (almost) any means necessary to help the parties reach an agreement, facilitative mediators do what they can to help the parties collaborate and problem-solve, drawing from a variety of tools to do so.

While the facilitative mediator likely believes that encouraging collaboration is the most effective way to help the parties reach an agreement, the mediator also considers the quality of the process, which they measure by the parties' behaviors. The facilitative mediator's version of a high-quality process is one where the parties are communicating respectfully, collaborating to solve problems, and making progress toward an agreement.

Transformative Mediation

Transformative mediators focus almost entirely on the goal of participating in a high-quality process, which they define solely by the mediator's behaviors. A transformative mediator who is participating in a high-quality process pays close attention to the parties, reflects them accurately, and supports their decisions, every step of the way.

Transformative mediators also value a high-quality outcome, which they define by the parties' empowerment shifts (where each party experiences a growing sense of strength and clarity) and recognition shifts (where each party experiences a growing understanding of the other). These shifts constitute an escape from the vicious circle of conflict, and are expected to flow naturally from the mediator's supportive interventions.

Understanding-Based Mediation

The understanding-based mediator prioritizes both the goal of helping the parties reach a high-quality outcome, and of participating in a high-quality process. As outcomes, the mediator aims for mutual understanding between the parties, in addition to an agreement that can meet each party's stated interests over time.

The understanding-based mediator measures the quality of the process by what the mediator and parties do together – to what extent is the mediator *looping* the parties effectively while leading them through the interest-based problem-solving steps? And to what extent are the parties making voluntary, informed decisions while participating in the stages of the process?

Narrative Mediation

The narrative mediator prioritizes both the quality of the outcome and the quality of the process. The narrative approach values an outcome that includes a cooperative, respectful relationship between the parties, along with respectful relations between each of the parties and others they may encounter in their homes, workplaces, and the larger society.

The narrative mediator's version of a high-quality process is one where the parties are communicating respectfully with each other and including the views of other affected parties, such as a company's employees or the children of a divorcing couple. The narrative mediator is particularly interested in amplifying the voices of members of groups the mediator sees as having less power.

AND THE WINNER IS...

If only it were that easy. It turns out research in this area is incredibly complicated (just think of all of the variables that would need to be held constant to compare one approach to the other!), so we cannot know, with certainty, which approach is more likely to lead to which outcomes (e.g., more agreements, "better" agreements, efficient resolutions, reduced conflict between the parties in the future, or more satisfied parties).[1]

Nonetheless, research has explored the effects of different strategies, or interventions, on the parties, with some suggestive results.[2] Of course, no strategy occurs in a vacuum, and the interventions may have interactive effects. For example, if a mediator directs the parties early in the process (such as by asking one party to speak first), this could give the parties the expectation that the mediator is in control. The parties may then play a more passive role in the process and rely on direction from the mediator going forward.[3] So, much is still unknown about the relative impacts of each approach on the parties, and on the mediator.

Since different approaches will appeal to different people, the trick is to find the one that's right for you. So where do you go from here? What are your next steps?

A FEW RECOMMENDATIONS

My first recommendation would be to do a deep dive into any approach that interests you. For the models, there is at least one foundational text, and often other books or chapters devoted to the model's theory and practice. All sources cited in this book are included in the reference list. I also put together a list of additional resources, including general mediation websites where you can find articles and videos covering a range of approaches (including interviews with mediators and demonstrations of different approaches), along with links to each mediation model's center or institute.

My second recommendation would be, take a mediator to lunch! While most mediators have a bias in favor of their preferred approach (even if their preferred approach is "eclectic"), they will generally be very happy to chat with an eager listener about something they're passionate about. And, in my experience, the vast majority of mediators are very passionate about their work!

Third, there's no substitute for being trained in an approach by someone who knows it well. While in-person trainings in each of the three mediation models are geographically limited, webinars and other online trainings may be available through each model's center or institute, or through other mediation organizations. If you'd like to learn the ins and outs of an approach, and certainly if you're considering practicing that way, investing the time and resources in a training (or two, or five, or...) would undoubtedly be worth your while.

Finally, know thyself. Which approach(es) would be a good match for your skills, abilities, natural inclinations, and educational background? And putting aside who you currently are, who do you *want* to be? Different approaches call for different attitudes and behaviors, which you may or may not want to strengthen in yourself.

For example, I have a natural tendency to try to solve everyone's problems. This tendency, as you can imagine, makes practicing the transformative approach challenging for me. But practicing this way also helps me become more the person I want to be – one who offers nonjudgmental support while trusting people to find their own answers. Although I respect other approaches, the transformative approach is most aligned with how I want to view and support others.

So thank you for taking the time to read about a topic I'm very passionate about. It's my firm belief that mediation can bring out the very best in people – clients and mediators alike – if all involved have found the right approach for them. It is my hope that this guide will be a helpful resource as you figure out which approach is right for you, paving your way to a successful and rewarding career as a mediator!

1   See Wall, J. A. & Dunne, T. C. (2012). Mediation research: A current review. *Negotiation Journal, 28*(2), 217-244.

2   See, e.g., Maryland Judiciary. (2016a). What works in child access mediation: Effectiveness of various mediation strategies on short-and long-term outcomes. Retrieved from https://mdcourts.gov/sites/default/files/import/courtoperations/pdfs/familyfullreport.pdf; Maryland Judiciary (2016b) What works in district court day of trial mediation: Effectiveness of various mediation strategies on short-and long-term outcomes. Retrieved from https://mdcourts.gov/sites/default/files/import/courtoperations/pdfs/districtcourtstrategiesfullreport.pdf; Wall, J. A., Dunne, T. C., & Chan-Serafin, S. (2011). The effects of neutral, evaluative, and pressing mediator strategies. *Conflict Resolution Quarterly, 29*(2), 127-150.

3   See Bush, R. A. B. (2019). A pluralistic approach to mediation ethics: Delivering on mediation's different promises. *Ohio State Journal on Dispute Resolution, 34*(3), 459-535.

REFERENCES

Abrams, P. Levy, R.L., Panay, A. (Producers), & Dobkin, D. (Director). (2005). *Wedding Crashers* [Motion Picture]. United States: New Line Cinema

American Arbitration Association, American Bar Association, and Association for Conflict Resolution (2005). Model standards of conduct for mediators. Retrieved from https://www.adr.org/sites/default/files/document_repository/AAA%20Mediators%20Model%20Standards%20of%20Conduct%2010.14.2010.pdf

American Bar Association Section of Dispute Resolution (2002). Mediation and the unauthorized practice of law. Retrieved from https://www.mediate.com/articles/abaupl.cfm

Beck, C. J. A., Sales, B. D., & Emery, R. E. (2004). Research on the impact of family mediation. In J. Folberg, A. L. Milne, & P. Salem (Eds.), *Divorce and family mediation* (pp. 447-482). New York: The Guildford Press.

Bertz, C., & Erickson, S. K. (2013, Winter). Response to Larry Gaughan's article. *The Professional Family Mediator*, pp. 4, 10. Retrieved from https://apfmnet.org/wp-content/uploads/APFM-newsletter-2013-Winter.pdf

Bickerman, J. (1996). Evaluative mediator responds. *Alternatives to the High Cost of Litigation, 14*(6), 70.

Bingham, L. B. (2012). Transformative mediation at the United States Postal Service. *Negotiation and Conflict Management Research, 5*(4), 354-366.

Bush, R. A. B. (2010). Taking self-determination seriously: The centrality of empowerment in transformative mediation. In J. P. Folger, R. A. B. Bush, & D. J. Della Noce (Eds.), *Transformative Mediation: A Sourcebook* (pp. 51-72). (n.p.): Institute for the Study of Conflict Transformation, Inc.

Bush, R. A. B. (2019). A pluralistic approach to mediation ethics: Delivering on mediation's different promises. *Ohio State Journal on Dispute Resolution, 34*(3), 459-535.

Bush, R. A. B., & Folger, J. P. (1994). *The promise of mediation: Responding to conflict through empowerment and recognition*. San Francisco, CA: Jossey-Bass.

Bush, R. A. B., & Folger, J. P. (2005). *The promise of mediation: The transformative approach to conflict.* San Francisco, CA: Jossey-Bass.

Bush, R. A. B., & Folger, J. P. (2012). Mediation and social justice: Risks and opportunities. *Ohio State Journal on Dispute Resolution, 27*(1), 1-51.

Bush, R. A. B., & Folger, J. P. (2013). Response to Condlin's critique of transformative mediation. *Cardozo Journal of Conflict Resolution, 15*(1), 231-241.

Bush, R. A. B. & Pope, S. G. (2002). Changing the quality of conflict interaction: The principles and practice of transformative mediation. *Pepperdine Dispute Resolution Law Journal, 3*(1), 67-96.

Catalyst IpF - Initiating Positive Futures. (2017, July 6). *Purple house conversations 2 of 2* [Video file]. Retrieved from https://www.youtube.com/watch?v=l5IZTIixtQk

Charkoudian, L. (2012). Just my approach: The practical, ethical, and empirical dangers of the lack of consensus about definitions of mediation approaches. *Negotiation and Conflict Management Research, 5*(4), 367-383.

Charkoudian, L., De Ritis, C., Buck, R., & Wilson, C. L. (2009). Mediation by any other name would smell as sweet—or would it? The struggle to define mediation and its various approaches. *Conflict Resolution Quarterly, 26*(3), 293-316.

Cleven, E. (2011).Who needs to talk to whom about what and wow? Transformative dialogue in settings of ethnopolitical conflict. *Institute for the Study of Conflict Transformation White Papers.*

Cooley, J. (2000). Defining the ethical limits of acceptable deception in mediation. Retrieved from https://www.mediate.com/articles/cooley1.cfm

Currie, C. (2000). Should a mediator also be an attorney? Retrieved from https://www.mediate.com/articles/currie.cfm

Della Noce, D. (2009). Evaluative mediation: In search of practice competencies. *Conflict Resolution Quarterly, 27*(2), 193-214.

Della Noce, D., Antes, J. R., & Saul, J. A. (2004). Identifying practice competence in transformative mediators: An interactive rating scale assessment model. *Ohio State Journal on Dispute Resolution, 19*(3), 1005-1058.

REFERENCES

Exon, S. N. (2006). How can a mediator be both impartial and fair: Why ethical standards of conduct create chaos for mediators. *Journal of Dispute Resolution, 2006*(2), 387-434.

Fisher, W., Ury, R. & Patton, B. (2011). *Getting to yes: Negotiating agreement without giving in.* New York, NY: Penguin Books.

Friedman, G. J. (1993). *A guide to divorce mediation: How to reach a fair, legal settlement at a fraction of the cost.* New York, NY: Workman Publishing.

Friedman, G. & Himmelstein, J. (2008). *Challenging conflict: Mediation through understanding.* Chicago, IL: American Bar Association.

George Carlin Quotes. (n.d.). BrainyQuote.com. Retrieved August 9, 2019, from BrainyQuote.com Web site: https://www.brainyquote.com/quotes/george_carlin_391403

Haynes, J. M. (1994). *The fundamentals of family mediation.* Albany: State University of New York Press.

Indiana Judicial Branch (n.d.). Mediation/Alternative Dispute Resolution. Retrieved from https://www.in.gov/judiciary/selfservice/2360.htm

Institute for the Study of Conflict Transformation, Inc. (2010). *Mediation: Principles & practice, the transformative approach* [training manual].

Kichaven, J. (2011). Use a mediator, get disbarred. Retrieved from https://jeffkichaven.com/wp-content/uploads/2017/10/GetDisbarredWebsite.pdf

Kovach, K. K. & Love, L. P. (1996, March). Evaluative mediation is an oxymoron. *CPR Institute for Dispute Resolution, 14*(3), 31-32.

Kressel, K. (2014). The mediation of conflict: Context, cognition, and practice. In P. T. Coleman, M. Deutsch, & E. C. Marcus (pp. 817-848), *The handbook of conflict resolution: Theory and practice.* San Francisco, CA: Jossey-Bass.

Kressel, K. & Wall, J. (2012). Introduction to the special issue on mediator approach. *Negotiation and Conflict Management Research, 5*(4), 334-339.

Love, L. (2011). Comments on cases 5.3 and 5.4. In E. Waldman (Ed.), *Mediation ethics: Cases and commentaries* (pp. 136-146). San Francisco, CA: Jossey-Bass.

Lowry, L. R. (2004). Evaluative mediation. In J. Folberg, A. L. Milne, & P. Salem (Eds.), *Divorce and family mediation* (pp. 72-91). New York: The Guildford Press.

Lundberg, D. & Moloney, L. (2010). Being in the room: Family dispute resolution practitioners' experience of high conflict family dispute resolution. *Journal of Family Studies, 16*(3), 209-223.

Malizia, D. A. & Jameson, J. K. (2018). Hidden in plain view: The impact of mediation on the mediator and implications for conflict resolution education. *Conflict Resolution Quarterly, 35*, 301-318.

Maryland Judiciary. (2016a). What works in child access mediation: Effectiveness of various mediation strategies on short-and long-term outcomes. Retrieved from https://mdcourts.gov/sites/default/files/import/courtoperations/pdfs/familyfullreport.pdf

Maryland Judiciary (2016b) What works in district court day of trial mediation: Effectiveness of various mediation strategies on short-and long-term outcomes. Retrieved from https://mdcourts.gov/sites/default/files/import/courtoperations/pdfs/districtcourtstrategiesfullreport.pdf

Mayer, B. (2004). Facilitative mediation. In J. Folberg, A. L. Milne, & P. Salem (Eds.), *Divorce and family mediation* (pp. 29-52). New York: The Guildford Press.

McDermott, E. P. (2012). Discovering the importance of mediator approach—An interdisciplinary challenge. *Negotiation and Conflict Management Research, 5*(4), 340-353.

Melamed, J. (2018). Sample mediation ground rules. Retrieved from https://www.mediate.com/articles/melamed7.cfm

Menkel-Meadow, C. (2011). Comments on case 12.2. In E. Waldman (Ed.), *Mediation ethics: Cases and commentaries* (pp. 320-327). San Francisco, CA: Jossey-Bass.

Milne, A. L., Folberg, J. & Salem, P. (2004). The evolution of divorce and family mediation. In J. Folberg, A. L. Milne, & P. Salem (Eds.), *Divorce and family mediation* (pp. 72-91). New York: The Guildford Press.

N.D. Ct. R. 8.8(a)(1)(A). Retrieved from https://www.ndcourts.gov/legal-resources/rules/ndrct/8-8

Neumann, D. (1996). *Choosing a divorce mediator: A guide to help divorcing couples find a competent mediator*. New York, NY: Henry Holt and Company.

REFERENCES

Nolan-Haley, J. (2011). Comments on cases 5.3 and 5.4. In E. Waldman (Ed.), *Mediation ethics: Cases and commentaries* (pp. 146-151). San Francisco, CA: Jossey-Bass.

Picard, C. A. (2004). Exploring an integrative framework for understanding mediation. *Conflict Resolution Quarterly, 21(3)*, 295-311.

Raines, S. S., Pokhrel, S. K., & Poitras, J. (2013). Mediation as a profession: Challenges that professional mediators face. *Conflict Resolution Quarterly, 21*(1), 79-97.

Riskin, L. (1994). Mediator orientations, strategies and techniques. *Alternatives to the High Cost of Litigation, 12*(9), 111–14.

Riskin, L. L. (1996). Understanding mediator orientations, strategies and techniques: A grid for the perplexed. *Harvard Negotiation Law Review, 1*(38), 1–51.

Riskin, L. L. (2003). Decision-making in mediation: The new old grid and the new grid system. *Notre Dame Law Review, 79*(1), 1-53.

Saposnek, D. T. (2004). Commentary: The future of the history of family mediation research. *Conflict Resolution Quarterly, 22*(1-2), 37-53.

Simon, D. (2010). Transformative mediation for divorce: Rising above the law and the settlement. In J. P. Folger, R. A. B. Bush, & D. J. Della Noce (Eds.), *Transformative Mediation: A Sourcebook* (pp. 249-270). (n.p.): Institute for the Study of Conflict Transformation, Inc.

Simon, D. (2012). Mediation redefined [blog post]. Retrieved from http://www.transformativemediation.org/mediation-redefined/

Simon, D. (n.d.). Old-school mediation techniques [blog post]. Retrieved from https://transformative-mediation.com/old-school-mediation/

Simon, D., West, T. (2019, July 24). Transformative mediation - Theory and practice [On-Demand CLE]. *American Bar Association, Section on Dispute Resolution*. Retrieved from https://www.americanbar.org/events-cle/ecd/ondemand/377910204/

Symposium on Standards of Practice for Family and Divorce Mediation Convened by the Association of Family and Conciliation Courts (2000). *Model standards of practice for family and divorce mediation.*

Retrieved from https://www.afccnet.org/Portals/0/PublicDocuments/CEFCP/ModelStandardsOfPracticeForFamilyAndDivorceMediation.pdf

Virginia's Judicial System (n.d.). Mediation. Retrieved from http://www.courts.state.va.us/courtadmin/aoc/djs/programs/drs/mediation/home.html

Waldman, E. (2011). *Mediation ethics: Cases and commentaries.* San Francisco, CA: Jossey-Bass.

Waldman, E. (1996). The challenge of certification: How to ensure mediator competence while preserving diversity. *University of San Francisco Law Review, 30*, 723-1281.

Wall, J. A. & Dunne, T. C. (2012). Mediation research: A current review. *Negotiation Journal, 28*(2), 217-244.

Wall, J. A., Dunne, T. C., & Chan-Serafin, S. (2011). The effects of neutral, evaluative, and pressing mediator strategies. *Conflict Resolution Quarterly, 29*(2), 127-150.

Wall, J. A. & Kressel, K. (2012). Research on mediator approach: A summary and some research suggestions. *Negotiation and Conflict Management Research, 5*(4), 403-421.

Welsh, N. (2001). The thinning vision of self-determination in court-connected mediation: The inevitable price of institutionalization? *Harvard Negotiation Law Review, 6*(1), 27-32.

Winslade, J. (2006). Mediation with a focus on discursive positioning. *Conflict Resolution Quarterly, 23*(4), 501-515.

Winslade, J. & Monk, G. (2001). *Narrative Mediation: A new approach to conflict resolution*. San Francisco, CA: Jossey-Bass.

ADDITIONAL RESOURCES

Mediate.com
https://www.mediate.com/

Mediator Academy
http://mediatoracademy.com/

Institute for the Study of Conflict Transformation
http://www.transformativemediation.org/

The Center for Understanding in Conflict
https://understandinginconflict.org/

Center for the Study of Narrative Analysis and Conflict Resolution
https://www.facebook.com/NarrativeAnalysis

ABOUT THE AUTHOR

Tara West lives in Asheville, North Carolina, and offers online mediation and conflict coaching to people anywhere in the world. She has studied facilitative, evaluative, understanding-based, and transformative approaches to mediation, and is certified as a transformative mediator by the Institute for the Study of Conflict Transformation. Tara earned her Ph.D. in Social and Health Psychology from Stony Brook University, and her Juris Doctor from the New York University School of Law. You can find her at www.tarawestmediation.com.

www.ingramcontent.com/pod-product-compliance
Lightning Source LLC
Chambersburg PA
CBHW060848220526
45466CB00003B/1279